GW01227554

THE AUSTRALIAN LIGHT HORSE

Light-horsemen stop for a smoke, and their horses for a nosebag, on the Philistine Plain in Palestine. Following the capture of Beersheba and Gaza, the British forces began their drive up the maritime plain and on to Jerusalem.

Australia
1788-1988

AUSTRALIANS AT WAR

THE AUSTRALIAN LIGHT HORSE

IAN JONES

TIME-LIFE BOOKS. AUSTRALIA
in association with JOHN FERGUSON. SYDNEY

Designed and produced by
John Ferguson Pty Ltd
100 Kippax Street
Surry Hills, NSW 2010

Editor: John Ferguson
Consulting Editor: George G. Daniels
Text Editor: Anthony Barker
Designer: Pamela Drewitt Smith
Picture Editor: Roger Williamson
Series Administrator: Lesley McKay
Production Manager: Ian MacArthur
Series Co-ordinator: Candace Campbell

Time-Life Books, South Pacific Books Division
Managing Director: Bonita L. Boezeman
Production Manager: Ken G. Hiley
Production Assistant: Jane Curry

The Author: IAN JONES is a journalist, scriptwriter and TV/Film producer-director with a special interest in the Australian Light Horse. He has delivered papers on aspects of the Light Horse at two Australian War Memorial History conferences and was appointed an honorary member of the 4th Light Horse Association at the 60th Anniversary pilgrimage to Gallipoli in 1975. Since then he has visited many of the battlegrounds of the light-horsemen in France, Egypt, Syria, Libya, Lebanon and Israel. Among other film/TV productions, he has written and produced the mini-series *Against the Wind* and *The Last Outlaw* and is screenwriter and co-producer of the feature film *The Lighthorsemen.*

First published in 1987 by
Time-Life Books (Australia) Pty Ltd
15 Blue Street
North Sydney, NSW 2060

© Time-Life Books (Australia) Pty Ltd 1987

This book is copyright. Apart from any fair dealing for the purposes of private study, research, criticism or review, as permitted under the Copyright Act, no part may be reproduced by any process without written permission. Inquiries should be addressed to the publisher.

National Library of Australia
cataloguing-in-publication data

Jones, Ian.
　The Australian Light Horse.

　Bibliography.
　Includes index.
　ISBN 0 949118 06 0
　1. Australia. Army. Australian Light Horse – History
　2. World War, 1914-1918 — Campaigns — Palestine.
　I. Title. (Series: Australians at war.).
940.4'15

This publication has been partially funded by the Australian Bicentennial Authority as part of its program to help celebrate Australia's Bicentennial in 1988.

Printed in Hong Kong

CONTENTS

Picture Essay		The Legend Begins	6
Chapter	1	**Raw Brigades**	**16**
		Saddling up for War	32
	2	**The Desert Column**	**44**
		Surviving in the Desert	66
	3	**The Charge at Beersheba**	**86**
		Shot in Colour	105
	4	**Deadlock in the East**	**114**
		The New Machines of War	136
	5	**The Great Ride**	**146**

Bibliography 164
Acknowledgments 165
Picture Credits 165
Index 166

THE LEGEND BEGINS

With the reins of his horse hitched over his arm, a member of the 5th South Australian Imperial Bushmen takes aim while a fellow trooper looks on.

"We went to South Africa as infantry, and they mounted us"

Two Bushmen of the 5th South Australian contingent display varying styles of uniform and general smartness. Trooper Ronald Easther (above) sits comfortably astride his fully equipped mount ready for action, while Trooper Wellington (below) presents an informal style more in keeping with the Australians' reputation.

BUSHMEN GUERRILLAS

When the Boer War broke out on October 11, 1899, Australia was still a group of separate British colonies, each of which offered a force to support Britain in her conflict with the Boers of the Transvaal and the Orange Free State. By the time the war was over, Australia had become a nation and had sent a total of 15,923 men to South Africa. With them went 16,314 horses; even the foot soldiers in time became mounted infantry.

War against the Boers demanded a new kind of fighting – guerrilla warfare, in which individuals and small groups acted on their own initiative. The Australian Bushmen excelled in this sort of fighting and even won praise from the Boers. Said a Boer historian: "Our men admitted that the Australians were formidable opponents and far more dangerous than any British troops."

They were also more of a rough-and-tumble lot, often helping themselves to supplementary rations from Boer farms and commandeering stock. As well, they caught and broke in hundreds of hardy veld ponies, which were better adapted to the local conditions than the Australian mounts.

Nevertheless, the Australian mounted forces served with distinction in South Africa. "All the colonials did extremely well," said Lord Roberts, Commander-in-Chief of the British forces. Six Victoria Crosses were awarded. At Elands River post in July 1900, a garrison consisting of 250 men of the Queensland Mounted Infantry and Victorian and New South Wales Bushmen held out for eight days against insuperable odds. When the Boer leader sent in a message inviting surrender, Colonel Hore, the British commander of the post, replied: "I cannot surrender.... I am in command of Australians who would cut my throat if I did." Lord Kitchener, who led in a force to relieve the Elands River post, remarked: "Only Colonials could have survived in such impossible circumstances."

The troopship Atlantian takes on horses for the New South Wales Citizen Bushmen's Contingent at Woolloomooloo in Sydney. The Atlantian sailed for South Africa on February 28, 1900, carrying 23 officers, 327 other ranks, 396 horses, and 11 carts and wagons.

Australian mounted troops cross a stream near Middelburg in the eastern Transvaal. Harry Chauvel, then a major, commanded a mixed force of Imperial and Queensland Mounted Infantry in the Middelburg district.

New South Wales Mounted Riflemen, rifles at the ready, cross the Orange River, which marked the southern boundary of the rebellious Orange Free State

With rifles stacked ready for use, Australian Bushmen make camp on the veld, and (right) others relax with a game of two-up. Though they lacked the discipline of British cavalry, the Australians were more self-reliant and could find their way about by day and by night over a largely featureless country.

Australian mounted infantrymen stand by their horses after a skirmish on the Modder River in the Orange Free State. The first Australian troops to arrive in South Africa were a group of 28 New South Wales Lancers who were training in Aldershot, England, when the war broke out.

Amid a stony and treeless landscape, Australian troops keep an eye on a Boer outpost.

Members of the New South Wales Imperial Bushmen round up two Boer prisoners.

A group of Boer guerrillas, a mixture of young and old, present a tough and determined appearance. Australian troops became adept in the kind of guerrilla tactics imposed by the Boers and the country itself.

Travelling in open railway wagons, men of the 5th South Australian Imperial Bushmen cross a bridge over the Modder River on their way to Cape Town to board a troopship on March 27, 1902, to take them home. From their arrival in 1901, the 5th had never been three consecutive days in the one place and had travelled 6,120 kilometres.

Lieutenant N. McGregor of the 3rd New South Wales Bushmen stands before a battlefield grave in the western Transvaal. Australian casualties were light in the Boer War, 251 being killed in action and 267 dying from illness.

1 RAW BRIGADES

The men who made the last great wartime cavalry charge were mounted infantry – Australian lighthorsemen. As "Bushmen" at the Boer War they had won high praise. At Gallipoli, dismounted, they fought gallantly and died tragically.

It was like a scene from the Crimea more than half a century before; officers on a hilltop with their folding chairs and tables, watching three lines of horsemen as they formed up to charge down a broad, shallow valley of naked rubble towards a formidable line of entrenchments and redoubts. Batteries of field guns were trained on that valley; machine-gunners and riflemen held high points along its rim, waiting for targets to appear. Two aircraft were arming with bombs and ammunition to repel any attack.

The sun was setting, and as the three fragile lines of horsemen moved out into the open in classic cavalry charge formation, it must have seemed that the end of this day would mark a bloody finale to the annals of mounted warfare. This was World War I, and already the Western Front had seen obscene mass slaughters of men and horses as 19th-century minds hurled cavalry against 20th-century weapons. On this 31st day of October, 1917, it was all but inevitable that the attack on Beersheba in Palestine would outdo these European insanities.

Yet this sunset charge against impossible odds would succeed – without even the losses any cavalry commander expected when he launched a charge. And these men who charged

"Raw-boned bush horse, in full marching order" — from George Lambert's sketchbook.

Beersheba were neither cavalry nor professional soldiers. They were Australian Light Horse – mounted infantry – citizen soldiers of the Australian Imperial Force which had been formed only three years before to join England in her war against Germany.

The men who rode into history that day straddled two ages. They had been born in the age of Queen Victoria; some of them rode horses broken to saddle by a man who had ridden with the Kelly Gang of bushrangers. And they carried the abilities of the frontier Australian into modern warfare with an ease that fascinated and baffled observers. They formed a fighting machine of an efficiency and audacity that staggered an enemy with a desert cavalry tradition of centuries. They matched the Bedouin in their ability to survive and thrive in the deserts and drylands. They fought with a terrible ferocity. Yet they remained gentle men.

In part, the men of the Light Horse typified the Australian soldier of World War I. But they showed qualities that marked them as unique even among other Australians of the time. And when their years of service were over, they melted back into the patterns of Australian life, scarcely understanding the legend they had created. The whole had become infinitely greater than its parts.

For the light-horseman, the harsh texture of daily survival – thirst, hunger, vermin, exhaustion and violent death – was an unglamorous reality. And despite the scope and scale of the legend they created, with its dash and audacity, its courage and endurance, the exploits of those tens of thousands of men and horses depended on one inescapable fact: a man riding a horse, carrying everything he needed for living and fighting – his clothing, his food and water, his horse's fodder, his ammunition, his weapons, his bedding, his shelter. Not for a comfortable weekend away from the creature comforts of home, but week in, week out, through blistering heat and bone-piercing cold, across some of the earth's harshest terrain. To grasp that is to begin to comprehend the story of the Australian Light Horse in World War I.

"We went to South Africa as infantry, and they mounted us. Now we come to North Africa as Light Horsemen, and they bundle us off as infantry." This remark, by "a philosophical Riverina grazier" about to leave for Gallipoli in May 1915, says much about the Light Horse. It captures their dry view of military wisdom, accurately conveys their dual role in two wars, and points out that they included men who had fought the formidable Boer commandoes.

In 1899, when the Australian colonies offered England a predominantly mounted force for the Boer War, the offer was regarded with a lofty disdain for amateur colonial cavalry. "Infantry, if possible" was the reply. But the colonies sent mainly horsemen anyway. Weeks after these "Bushmen" arrived in South Africa and the first impact of their unmilitary behaviour had faded, their abilities won extravagant praise from English officers and observers. Even the Australian infantry were provided with horses, and the colonial governments were told, without a blush, "Her Majesty's Government requires an additional force of 2,000 men of a similar kind to the Bushmen."

Mounted units dominated the old colonial militias, achieving a popularity and glamour very different from the élitist traditions of British cavalry. They were seen as the military expression of qualities and abilities that were still basic to almost every level of Australian rural life and equally cherished by city dwellers. The horsemanship of the Bushmen was a mere starting point – essential, but as basic as an infantryman's ability to walk and run. They were used to a self-sufficient outdoor life, making do with little food and water – though perhaps rather more than legend acknowledges – working in a remarkable variety of landforms and climates. They had grown up with firearms as a part of everyday life. They showed a gift for navigation that went beyond map-reading and memorising landmarks to become a total sense of terrain. And they had a feel for movement and survival in any tract of land, giving them ability to exploit its features in attack and defence.

Most remarkably, each man and his horse were a fighting unit that could operate independently or mesh in with section, troop, squadron or regiment. To the English, it often seemed strange that men who thrived on isolation could team so effectively. But it was a natural outgrowth of the way they had lived and worked. They were often alone for weeks and months, making their own decisions, improvising, surviving. But when it was needed and available, teamwork became all the more highly valued. and, under the threats and pressures of frontier life, reliance on team-mates was absolute. This was, in fact, the core of the much-discussed bush mateship: mutual interdependence when the going was rough. There was another factor which defied analysis: something between the man and the horse, more than trust and affection and devotion, a sense of mutual destiny.

In the debacle of the Boer War – 450,000 British and colonial troops taking three years to defeat less than 22,000 Boers – the Australian mounted infantry leapt to prominence. A Boer wrote: "Our men admitted that the Australians were more formidable opponents and far more dangerous than the British troops." The British Commander-in-Chief, Lord Roberts, was quite besotted with the Australians' horsemanship, and even Lord Kitchener expressed gruff admiration for their tenacity and ability to succeed against impossible odds.

True, their attitude toward discipline was something of a problem. When youngish Major Edmund Allenby of England's crack Inniskilling Dragoons took over a squadron of the New South Wales Lancers, both the Lancers and Allenby wondered what had struck them. But each learnt something of the other's ways, and while the squadron became spit-and-polish in the Inniskilling tradition, Allenby found new dimensions to his ideas of discipline. Yet he remained Allenby, and when some of his squadron appeared with *A.O.V.* – for "Allenby's Own Volunteers" – written in indelible pencil on their hats, he fined them for destroying Her Majesty's property. Sixteen years later, when he was a knighted general, Allenby would have all the Light Horse in Palestine under his command.

Among the Australians' harshest critics was one of their own officers in South Africa, Major Harry Chauvel of the Queensland Mounted Infantry – who, as General Sir Harry Chauvel, would become another giant figure in the greater war to come. This dapper little professional deplored the failings of some of his men – not small things like failing to salute, but such serious breaches as straggling, malingering, even shirking action – all "un-Australian" yet all present on occasion in South Africa. To Chauvel, the solution lay in the calibre and style of officering and the creation of an esprit de corps. On his return to Australia, now a newborn Commonwealth, he campaigned energetically to achieve these aims.

Another Boer War Officer, Major-General Sir Edward Hutton, would have an enormous impact on Australia's mounted troops. This volatile man was a dogged advocate of the mounted infantry style of fighting, and on becoming the first Commander-in-Chief of the Australian army in 1901, he saw to it that the Light Horse of the young Commonwealth would gain full benefit from the lessons of the Boer War.

Given new impetus by the compulsory military training scheme of 1901, the Light Horse flourished, and by 1914 there were 23 regiments scattered throughout the broad land. That year, England's General Sir Ian Hamilton inspected the citizen army and pronounced the Light Horse as "the pick of the bunch," still less disciplined, he thought, than British cavalry, but showing more initiative and, in his hearty estimation, "real thrusters."

So, in the first days of August 1914, Australia waited eagerly for England to declare war on Germany. This would be the young Commonwealth's chance to prove itself. Liberal and Labour – in the throes of a political deadlock that led to double dissolution and a federal election – outdid each other in expressions of loyalty to "the Mother Country." A writer of the time noted that "men went about the great Australian cities in a kind of feverish dream." The same dream gripped the smallest country town and the spaces beyond. By the time war was declared on August 4, Prime Minister Joseph Cook had promised 20,000 troops to Britain, including a Light Horse brigade of 2,226 men.

In the early stages of war, volunteers could nominate their branch of service, and men flocked to join the Light Horse as a focus of Australian ideals. In the romantic description of Henry Gullett, official historian of the Light Horse in Sinai and Palestine, there were "dairymen and small cultivators from the long rich coastal belt between the Dividing Range and the sea; orchardists from the foot-hills; timber-getters from the sparkling forests on the ranges; men from the larger farms of the long wheat belt, on the inside slope of the mountains; and men whose lives had been spent on the sheep and cattle stations of the vast inland plains." But there were also butchers and building contractors and floorwalkers and confectioners and publicans. In fact, nearly 20 per cent of the Light Horse would come from the cities. Of the two scouts galloping ahead of the charge at Beersheba, one would be a station hand, the other a suburban carpenter. Continued Gullett: "Every worn road and grass-grown track carried its eager, excited volunteers, some riding singly, some in twos and threes. Squatters and stockmen and shearers, farmers and labourers and prospectors, they paced the same road in the spirit of true democracy, which, as the war went on, became

KANGAROO FEATHERS

When the Australian Light Horse was formed in 1914, Queenslanders, Tasmanians and South Australians wore emu plumes in their hats—patches of emu hide with the long, flowing feathers still attached. The emu plume had originally been a battle honour of the Queensland Mounted Infantry for their work in the shearers' strike of 1891. It was quickly adopted by almost all the Light Horse regiments in Egypt—much to the indignation of some Queenslanders—and became the badge of the Light Horseman, soon to become known to the Turks on the Gallipoli peninsula. A prisoner in the Sinai said to his emu-plumed guard, "You Australian bird, same Gallipoli."

The Arabs called the Light Horse "the Kings of the Feathers," a name that captured the curious dignity the shower of plumes gave to the most battered hat and denoted the fierce pride with which they came to be worn. Yet, as with most things he cared about, the light-horseman spoke little of his crest. Asked about it, he would say they were "kangaroo feathers." But let any man ridicule the fashion, and he had a fight on his hands.

When Scots artillerymen were attached to the Light Horse, they asked permission to wear emu-plumed hats. It was the British army that refused. The Light Horse had no objections. They could have offered no greater compliment to their comrades in arms.

perhaps the most beautiful and valuable of all the great qualities that in this war shone out of the Australian soldier."

But when they arrived in staging camps and the first regiments took shape, men would discover that rural hierarchy had been transferred into the army. Although the Australian Imperial Force was created especially for First World War service, most officers of the citizen Light Horse units carried their ranks into the new army. They were usually graziers, employers and professional men. As a policy, men of the same district were initially grouped in a squadron, men of the same town in a troop. So, a big grazier would have his stockmen and contractors under his command; a doctor or dentist would officer his patients; a country racehorse owner might have his jockey as a batman. A familiar sort of colonial feudalism balanced the egalitarianism that would develop during the war – and helped ease the transition to a military life.

Many men brought their own horses, which, if accepted by government inspectors, were bought by the Commonwealth. Most men, however, were issued with remounts – army horses, popularly called "walers" (short for New South Walers) – which could range from near-outlaws to well-trained stock horses and thoroughbreds. Shrewd bushmen looked for the brands of stations with a good reputation. An officer wryly recalled: "It was not child's play tackling some of those horses. Some of the kind-hearted station folk in the backblocks had sent down some wild warrigals of the west; bucking brumbies that beat the band; old outlaws off the grass that the station hands could never master." Wild, mud-spattering rodeos erupted in camps all over Australia. But, as the same officer commented, "the bush boys stuck to the saddles as the Old Man of the Sea stuck to Sindbad the Sailor, and one after another the bucking brumbies were broken and led away."

Mounting the Light Horse Brigade took weeks while the Government Harness Factory at Clifton Hill, near Melbourne, raced to complete saddles and leatherwork. Meanwhile, men thronged the training camps in rag-tag-and-bobtail mixtures of civilian dress, militia uniform and AIF fatigues – dungaree pants and dungaree "butchers' coats."

Men slept in bell tents, eight or ten to a tent, feet to the centre pole. It was mid-winter, and in the first days some recruits had only a groundsheet on the bare, cold earth. Luckier ones could pack straw under their hips. There was a Wild West air about those early camps. Some men had brought their dogs as well as their horses, thought it appropriate to carry revolvers, moved everywhere at the gallop, and grazed their horses on any grass or crop in sight. But men and horses quickly shook down into a military routine, the walers tethered by head and heel ropes between long picket lines which were guarded all night by sentries.

The militarisation of the horses seemed to demand a matching discipline from the men. At the crack of dawn, reveille roused them to "stables" – cleaning the lines and watering and feeding their horses before breakfast. Then came training. Most men were already capable horsemen and good shots. But a quarter of them had never received any form of military training. So, in an intensive few weeks, discipline and Light Horse drill were hammered into them all by NCOs of the professional army.

The Light Horse Brigade (called the "1st" Brigade by General W.T. Bridges, the far-sighted Commander-in-Chief of the AIF) comprised three regiments – the 1st Australian Light Horse Regiment raised in New South Wales, the 2nd Regiment from Queensland, and the 3rd Regiment from South Australia and Tasmania. A 4th Regiment was recruited in Victoria as divisional cavalry for the 1st Infantry Division.

In temporary command of the 1st Brigade was Lieutenant-Colonel J.K. Forsyth, who was also commanding officer of the 4th Light Horse Regiment. This forgotten father of the Light Horse – a small, devoutly religious teetotaller – shared Chauvel's background in the Queensland Mounted Infantry and also his passion for discipline. But Forsyth had not seen action in South Africa, so he could remain a military romantic

THE AUSTRALIAN WARHORSE

The men of the Light Horse rode standard Australian stockhorses, regarded by English officers as "rather on the light side." Yet one of these officers would write, "Their record in this war places them far above the cavalry horses of any other nation."

Since the 1830s, a healthy trade had been built up in the export of Australian horses to the British army in India – New South Wales stockhorse types, dubbed "walers." Australian horses probably took part in the charge of the Light Brigade in 1854; they won many laurels in Britain's native wars of the 19th century and the calamitous Boer War. But it was in World War I that the waler stunned the military world.

The classic waler was 15 to 16 hands (although many were 14 to 15 hands), sired by an English thoroughbred from breeding mares that were part draught horse. The Welsh pony, Timor pony and brumby, with their hardiness and stamina, often contributed to the waler's conformation, defined by a Light Horse veterinary officer as "fine clean legs and bone, with a short back, large barrel, fine neck and broad head." Used as a stockhorse, the waler could be ridden day after day mustering cattle and, at night, simply unsaddled and turned out to look after itself.

Australian horses could travel faster and farther than the heavier, coarser breeds favoured by England and other cavalry nations. They ate and drank less, rarely collapsed from exhaustion, and recovered quickly. Eventually carrying loads of more than 130 kilograms, they would travel 80 kilometres a day, often through searing heat, sometimes going 60 and 70 hours without a drink, yet still able to produce bursts of remarkable speed.

One 16-hand chestnut, known as Bill the Bastard because of a habit of bucking, carried five men at a labouring gallop over soft sand for more than a kilometre when the Turks overran their outpost during the battle of Romani. Two men were mounted behind the regular rider, and the other two were on either side standing on a stirrup and hanging on. It was the only time that Bill the Bastard was known to gallop without first bucking. The gallant horse was never again required to carry a rider and served out the remainder of the war as an officer's packhorse.

By the end of the war, 160,000 Australian horses had been sent overseas. Only one returned – Sandy, the charger of Major-General Sir William Bridges, Commander-in-Chief of the AIF. When Bridges was killed at Gallipoli, Sandy was shipped back to Australia to be led with empty saddle at his funeral. Sandy's head is preserved in the Australian War Memorial in Canberra.

A most effective memorial to the waler can also be found there – in the Light Horse paintings of George W. Lambert. A light-horseman commented: "He portrayed them more faithfully than any camera because he captured their spirit and the light in their eyes."

Two of the original Light Horse walers of the AIF, with their riders in the saddle, parade before departure from Australia.

and dream of the Light Horse carrying out some fabulous exploit like the charge of the 21st Lancers at Omdurman.

Forsyth's own regiment exemplified Chauvel's ideal of esprit de corps. It became an extended family, his men actually referring to him as "Dad". Although he had hand-picked his 546 men from Victoria's first 2,000 Light Horse volunteers, there were still plenty of hard cases among them. Yet the core of the regiment's spit-and-polish tradition and high standard of discipline was a simple desire to satisfy "Dad".

The regiments were steadily equipped, mounted and uniformed. Khaki cloth and polished brown leather replaced the tatterdemalion of the early weeks. In remarkably short time, the light-horsemen emerged as an élite of the AIF—easily picked out by their leather bandoliers, leather belts, leather leggings, and spurs, moving with the swagger of natural-born winners and already the best-disciplined branch of the army. They were eager to match themselves against British cavalry on the Western Front, shielded as they were by a propagandist press from ugly truths that were already evident. Cavalry—British, French, Belgian and German—were being slaughtered in their hundreds. But British senior officers with hunt club mentalities were staunch in their belief that cavalry could still triumph. They were eager to hurl the Australian Light Horse into the hellholes of France and Flanders.

Meanwhile, in a heady brew of high adventure, semi-religious patriotism and knockabout farce, the 1st Brigade was shaped, a second was recruited, then a third and the basis of a fourth. Within seven months, 8,000 light-horsemen would be at Britain's disposal.

In October 1914, the battalions of the 1st Division and the regiments of the 1st Light Horse Brigade embarked from their home ports to rendezvous with the New Zealand contingent in the superb Princess Royal Harbour at Albany, Western Australia. On Sunday, November 1, the fleet sailed for England—three cruisers escorting 36 transports in three lines, each 12 kilometres long, a proud spectacle.

The first day out, they received news that

The Australian Governor-General, Sir Ronald Munro-Ferguson, inspects the 1st Light Horse Regiment of the Australian Imperial Force before its departure for Egypt.

England had declared war on Turkey. It seemed a minor detail of the war. Not even the keenest strategic brain could predict the profound effect this would have on the men of the AIF. The following day, the fleet picked up two more transports with another cruiser and forged out across the Indian Ocean.

While the infantry trained and exercised like tourists in their blue dungarees, sandshoes and white canvas hats, the men of the Light Horse worked almost desperately to keep their horses fit. Each day they had to "muck out" the stalls, rub down their walers and, where possible, exercise them on deck, leading them up wooden ramps covered with coir matting. Captain Jack Hindhaugh of the 1st Brigade staff was on the transport *Wiltshire*. He wrote in his diary: "This is a bad boat for horses, no ventilation and not able to hose out the decks. Am afraid we will lose a lot of them, poor beggars. They are on five decks, two above and three below [the water line]. The bottom deck is called 'Little Hell' and is a terror."

By November 6, across the Tropic of Capricorn, it was getting hotter, and seven horses had already died on the *Wiltshire*. Hindhaugh noted grimly; "At this rate, we won't have many horses left by the time we land in England." But the troopers worked all the harder for the awful conditions, spending every spare moment with their horses, grooming them and easing their torture. In "Little Hell" and every other airless lower deck of the Light Horse transports, men stripped to their shorts and slaved for hours with brushes, curry-combs and canvas buckets of water. Most horses endured it silently, heads low in the feebly lit stalls. Some moaned and whinnied. The men suffered with them, giving what comfort they could, helping develop and strengthen the remarkable relationship which would carry man and horse through the years ahead.

Of the 497 walers aboard the *Wiltshire*, 484 would come through the voyage in excellent condition. It represented a remarkable achievement, matched by the other Light Horse transports, which lost only about three per cent of their horses in seven weeks at sea.

On November 28, a rumour swept the fleet that the men of the AIF would disembark in Egypt and complete their training there, instead of in England. It proved to be true. Harry Chauvel, now a lieutenant-colonel, had been in England as Australian representative to the War Office. He found the proposed training camp on Salisbury Plain totally unsuitable and campaigned to have the AIF trained in Egypt while the European winter passed and the English camp was brought up to scratch. The proposal went through, and Chauvel sailed for Egypt to take command of the 1st Light Horse Brigade, unaware of the momentous impact this change of plan would have on the Australian troops.

Men and horses began disembarking at Alexandria on December 3 and travelled to Cairo by train. Some of the Light Horse were with the infantry in Mena Camp at the foot of the pyramids, some at Maadi, a few kilometres south: others would soon move into camp at nearby Heliopolis. Forsyth handed over the 1st Brigade to Chauvel and took command of his own regiment; intensive training started.

Chauvel quickly showed an almost obsessive desire to bring his brigade up to English standards of drill and discipline. It was odd to see this wiry little country man seemingly hell-bent on making Horse Guards out of bushmen. Interestingly, his predecessor, the city-bred Forsyth, had given every original member of his regiment a cased stockman's quartpot (a combined mug and billy), because he considered the British cavalry mess tin unpractical. It was symbolic that, through the coming years, the mess tin steadily vanished from the everyday use of the Light Horse. Their preference for the stockman's billycan, quartpot and enamel plate marked a return to the very practicalities of bush life that carried the light-horseman to his unique place in military history.

For the time being, however, British straight backs and spit-and-polish prevailed. Certainly this was so in Chauvel's 1st Brigade and in the 3rd Brigade, which was commanded by Colonel G.F. Hughes, an elderly Melbourne businessman well known in social circles—a thoroughly respectable officer—with Lieutenant-Colonel J.M. Antill, a ramrod-lean, veteran of the Boer War, as his brigade major.

The 2nd Brigade was something of a problem in those early days. It was under Colonel Granville Ryrie, regarded as an unknown quantity by the high command. And no wonder, Ryrie was an unlikely figure—a grazier, heavyweight boxer and federal parliamentarian, who tipped the scales at more than 100 kilograms and radiated easygoing *bonhomie*. But he was also a consummate horseman and a born leader, totally adored by his men. At first there were questions of discipline, but in the end his brigade would prove its mettle in combat. As historian Henry Gullett discreetly put it: "He was more successful in the field than in the training camp."

After their time at sea, the horses could not be ridden immediately. They were exercised daily for about 12 days and then reintroduced to mounting and dismounting before being ridden at the walk for only 15 minutes, for half an hour the next day, and so on. Soon, men and horses were exercising by troop, squadron and regiment in the rolling sand dunes on the edge of the Sahara. For the first time, officers and men could glimpse the remarkable spectacle of mass mounted action—a regiment in squadron line abreast, a brigade in column of route, four abreast, cavalcading across the sea of sand.

When he was satisfied with his men's progress in mounted infantry drill, Forsyth indulged his cavalry dreams and drilled the men of the 4th Light Horse Regiment in the classic knee-to-knee cavalry charge, drawing their bayonets and flourishing them like swords. He delighted visiting French and Russian generals with a spectacular display of the manoeuvre. But when the 4th repeated the charge in a mock battle

---

ORDER OF BATTLE

AUSTRALIAN LIGHT HORSE

1st Brigade
1st Regiment (NSW)
2nd Regiment (Qld)
3rd Regiment (SA and Tas.)

2nd Brigade
5th Regiment (Qld)
6th Regiment (NSW)
7th Regiment (NSW)

3rd Brigade
8th Regiment (Vic.)
9th Regiment (SA and Vic.)
10th Regiment (WA)

4th Brigade
4th Regiment (Vic.)
11th Regiment (Qld and SA)
12th Regiment (NSW)

5th Brigade
14th Regiment (from Imperial Camel Corps)
15th Regiment (from Imperial Camel Corps)
French colonial regiment (Spahis and Chasseurs d'Afrique)

A regiment consisted of about 500 men formed into three squadrons; a squadron was made up of four troops; a troop had 10 sections, with four men in each section.

DESERT COLUMN
(Sinai, February 1917)

Anzac Mounted Division
1st Australian Light Horse Brigade
2nd Australian Light Horse Brigade
New Zealand Mounted Rifles Brigade

Imperial Mounted Division
3rd Australian Light Horse Brigade
4th Australian Light Horse Brigade
5th Yeomanry Brigade
6th Yeomanry Brigade

DESERT MOUNTED CORPS
(Allenby Reorganisation, August 1917)

Anzac Mounted Division

Australian Mounted Division
3rd Australian Light Horse Brigade
4th Australian Light Horse Brigade

Imperial Camel Corps

Yeomanry Mounted Division

AUSTRALIAN MOUNTED DIVISION
(Palestine, 1918)

3rd Australian Light Horse Brigade
4th Australian Light Horse Brigade
5th Australian Light Horse Brigade

with Australian infantry, indignant referees pronounced almost 100 per cent casualties from machine-gun fire. Everyone knew that a mounted charge was impossible against modern weaponry. Everyone, that is, except Forsyth, the men who rode in those crazy charges, and, just possibly, the infantrymen who faced them.

On December 18, a 101-gun salute had been fired in Cairo to signal the establishment of a British protectorate in Egypt. It was England's attempt to solve one of the unusual problems created by Turkey's entry into the war as an ally of Germany. The Turkish move had coincided with a call by the Turkish Sultan—who was also the leader of worldwide Islam—for a jehad, a holy war against the infidel. His spiritual subjects included the Muslims of Egypt, whose north-eastern borders met Palestine, a Turkish possession for 400 years. And through Egypt ran the Suez Canal, a vital artery of the war.

England's early reverses on the Western Front had encouraged a volatile blend of Islamic fervour and Egyptian nationalism. When a British territorial division marched into Cairo, the natives saw, in the words of the British official correspondent, W.T. Massey, "a division of half-trained and not too well equipped men ... mill workers and miners, many of them, whose daily labour had made them pale of cheek." The people of Cairo were openly derisive.

But when the first Australians and New Zealanders arrived, Massey noted how "their physique and 'stand no nonsense' attitude greatly impressed the people." General Sir John Maxwell, commanding the forces in Egypt, could breathe more easily. Not only did he now control a force that could meet any Turkish threat to the Suez Canal, but he had the means to supress the simmer of Islamic/nationalist rebellion. The dominion troops were tacitly encouraged to assume the role of guard dogs over the Muslim masses. Not that they ever needed much urging.

From their first encounter with Egyptians in Port Said, the Australians had developed a remarkable antipathy towards them. They considered them dishonest, dirty, cruel to animals, and exploiters of their womenfolk. The Egyptians, in turn, regarded the Australians as infidels and, as such, subjects for exploitation and pillage. Certainly, Australians and Egyptians seemed to bring out the worst in each other. The Light Horse, like other Australian soldiers, unmercifully baited dealers in the bazaars. A Light Horse officer noted the following exchange:

"Five pounds for one beautiful scarab."

"Ha ha!"

"Not ha ha! It is three thousand years old! Time of Rameses the Second."

"Too old. Got any nice new ones?"

And there were the signs: "Don't go elsewhere to be cheated, Australians. Come here!" and the immortal "English and French spoken; Australian understood."

Cairo's notorious red light district in the Haret el Wasser—a street known to the troops as "the Wozza"—saw a spectacular riot between Australians, New Zealanders and the Cairo populace, in which several buildings were burnt and a grand piano was pushed out through a casement window onto a hostile crowd. Light Horse helped subdue the trouble, This was on Good Friday, April 2, 1915. The following night, Mena Camp at the foot of the pyramids blazed with hundreds of bonfires as the 1st Division prepared to embark for Gallipoli, leaving the 4th Light Horse Regiment and the newly arrived 3rd Light Horse Brigade in camp—along with two infantry mascot wallabies which hopped into the picket lines one night and stampeded some of the walers.

News of the landing at Anzac and the beginnings of the stalemated Gallipoli campaign arrived with the Red Crescent trains that steamed into Cairo carrying wounded. A lighthorseman wrote: "When we saw our fellows coming back with their wounds upon them—when we heard of what they had been through—when we listened to their story of that wonderful landing on Gallipoli on April 25, and of the wild charge they made up the frowning hill—all of us, to a man, begged to be sent to the front as infantry." Regiment by regiment, brigade by brigade, they volunteered to leave their beloved horses in Egypt and join the "gravel crushers" they pretended to despise.

General Sir Ian Hamilton, in command on Gallipoli, wanted the Light Horse as drafts and reinforcements. General Maxwell, in Egypt, did not want his troops there whittled away and scattered. But then, Hamilton did not want what he called "raw brigades." Eventually, the Light Horse were sent as intact units to fight as infantry. Dad Forsyth was heartbroken. His dream of an élite cavalry regiment would be destroyed by attrition – casualties being replaced by whatever reinforcements were available. Nevertheless, as a good soldier, he accepted a posting as assistant adjutant and quartermaster-general to the 1st Infantry Division and sailed for Anzac. His regiment and the three Light Horse brigades would soon follow.

The amazing Anzac beach-head was scarcely three weeks old when the 1st Light Horse Brigade started landing on May 12. The 2nd and 3rd Brigades would follow in a week, waiting to land while the 1st Brigade helped beat back the huge Turkish attack of May 19, with the loss of 131 men in the action.

The first impression was Anzac Cove itself – the narrow, stony beach crowded with stores, and the scrubby yellow clay hills rising sheer behind it. Already, in the warming spring days, men were swimming in the calm waters of the cove. Then came the climb up Shrapnel Gully, a scrubby ravine that cut from the right-hand end of the beach up into a bewildering tangle of eroded ridges and gullies peppered with dugouts and shelters. When the newly arrived troopers ducked at the whistle of a bullet overhead, the old hands of the infantry laughed and said, "They're only canaries."

Trooper Humphrey Kempe of the 3rd Light Horse Regiment studied these "veterans" as he passed. "To us, these soldiers of only two weeks' battle experience looked strangely drawn with grey faces of fatigue and shock and grey uniforms dusty from close contact with clays of shallow scrapes and dugouts. I remember being struck with their unsmiling unshaven gravity, sure of themselves, but to our sharpened sense carrying a look in their faces touched with strokes of the old religious representations of Christ."

A gully forked off to the right. This was Monash Valley, a highway to the heart of the Anzac battleground, narrowing steeply to the Nek, a causeway ridge of scrubby no man's land between the highest Australian trenches on the left and the higher Turkish positions on the right. Along the rim of Monash Valley's cliff-like right-hand slope were several of the major Australian posts – Pope's, Quinn's, Courtney's and Steele's – key forward posts in the ragged crescent of trenches that marked the first day's toe-hold on Turkish soil. Most light-horsemen were put to digging their "possies" in these dangerous slopes. Others would make their homes out to the right on a level bench called Shell Green.

Food was plentiful but boring; however, water was scarce. The newcomers were quickly infested with fleas and lice, and they learnt to live with the smell of death. Some of the front-line trenches had bodies of Australians killed on the first day built into their parapets. Almost every day, digging a trench or possie, men unearthed hurriedly buried Turks.

With a high proportion of country men, the Light Horse adapted readily to the appalling living conditions. They quickly swung into the routine of digging, lugging rations and water up from the beach, waiting in support and reserve trenches, and taking their turn in the firing line. Here, the major threat, apart from occasional Turkish attacks, was from mines planted by tunnellers and Turkish "cricket ball" bombs – a special menace at Quinn's Post, which came within 15 metres of the Turkish front line. In one particularly heavy bomb attack, Trooper Kempe had been the only man left in the post. As he described the hideous scene: "Tinned bully beef lying on the floor of the trench, together with uniform and web equipment, had been blown into the clay walls of the trench. They were speckled with meat and khaki. A blue scarf left behind was more holes than wool, while the body of a Turk built into the trench wall

Taken from Steele's Post, this view of the Anzac area looks across rugged terrain to Shrapnel Gully and Monash Valley. The map below shows Anzac Cove and the main battle area of the Australian and New Zealand forces on Gallipoli.

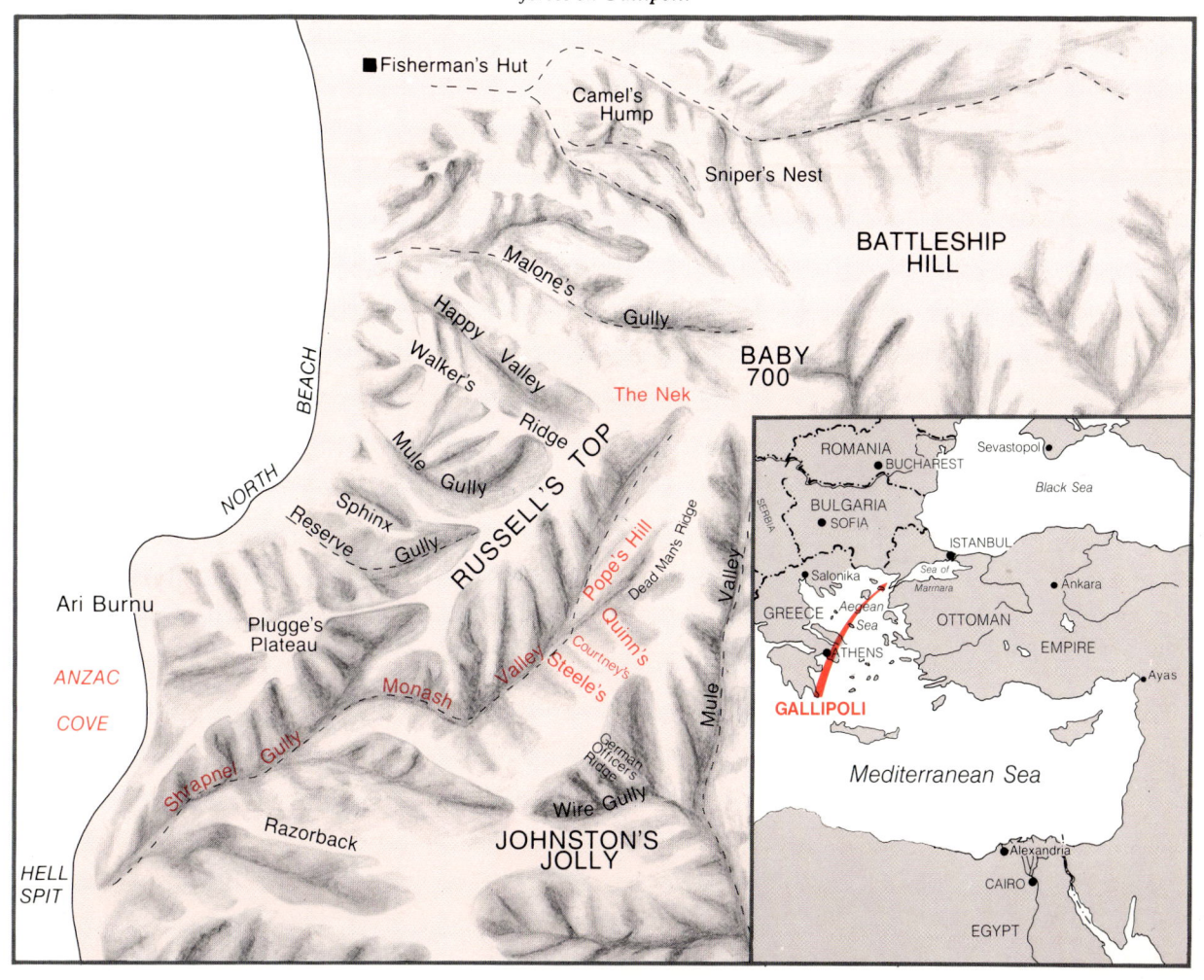

showing only a pair of huge soles had sprung a long leak of indescribable matter." Here, as Kempe noted, "the air was thick with bullets, so much so that some sandbags on parapets held more ammunition than soil."

The deep trenches, cut in key patterns, were comparatively safe from the shrapnel shells that exploded in mid-air and blasted dozens of bullets down at a sharp angle like some giant shotgun. Anywhere on the beach-head, shrapnel could strike, every hour of the day and night. A trooper wrote in his diary, "No matter on what peaceful errand we go, death goes too. We never know whether we will wake up alive."

The tracks between the beach and the bivouac areas were a shooting gallery for Turkish snipers until a special squad of sharpshooters was raised from the Light Horse brigades. They quickly reduced the sniper menace and then turned their attention to the front line. Trooper Billy Sing of the 5th Light Horse Regiment became famous, nicknamed "the Murderer" by his mates. Using an observer with a telescope, he shot more than 150 Turks. Another crack Light Horse sniper was Sergeant Brennan of the 7th Light Horse field kitchen. Each day after breakfast he would stroll to the firing line and lure a Turkish sniper into a duel.

The Great Adventure was slow to sour for some of the newly arrived light-horsemen. One wrote on May 28: "Just as I walked out of my dug-out this morning two men were shot by a machine gun not ten yards off – one in the shoulder and the other in the eye. Ten seconds ago a big shrapnel shell burst right in front of our dug-out. The bullets flew everywhere and we bolted for shelter. Up to the present it has been the most wonderful week of my life – full of excitement and hair-breadth escapes."

The writer was Lieutenant Oliver Hogue, orderly to the remarkable Colonel Ryrie, who had his own share of escapes. During a Turkish bombardment of Shell Green, several men were hit and Ryrie left his headquarters dugout to investigate. A shrapnel shell exploded near by; in the hush after the burst, Ryrie remarked cheerily, "Holy Moses, they've got me where the chicken got the axe." A shrapnel pellet had entered his neck and stopped just short of the carotid artery. He was evacuated but later returned to Anzac. Many light-horsemen were less lucky. Soon, Lieutenant Hogue would be writing, "You saw old pals in the morning and you didn't see them in the evening . . . and then you realised what a thin line it is that separates life from death."

That thin line stretched to breaking point in August, the month of a huge Allied offensive against the Turks. On the night of August 6, a major landing of British troops a few miles north at Suvla Bay would integrate with an Anzac assault on the commanding height of Chunuk Bair. Earlier in the evening, an Australian attack on the Turkish-held Lone Pine plateau would draw attention from this crucial strike. The following dawn the Light Horse would play the key role in a series of feints to aid the attack on Chunuk Bair and, theoretically, be supported by that attack.

In the cold light of hindsight, the whole plan seems a framework of unmatched pieces. Enormous responsibility rested on raw troops of Kitchener's new army under the elderly General Sir Frederick Stopford, who was Lieutenant of the Tower of London before the war and had never led men in action. In the dawn feints of August 7, the 3rd Light Horse Brigade, comprising the 8th, 9th and 10th Regiments, was given the daunting task of charging across the Nek – the causeway ridge at the head of Monash Valley – to attack nine tiers of Turkish trenches on rising ground. The Nek was so narrow that only 150 men could form up abreast, so the 900 riflemen of the brigade would charge in six lines or waves. The three regiments drew lots for the honour of the charge – and the 8th Regiment won. They would make up the first and second waves. The 10th Regiment would be in the third and fourth lines, the 9th Regiment in the fifth and sixth reserve lines. Orders promised "the full strength of naval guns and high explosive fire from the full strength of our howitzer and other guns."

Men were to discard tunics and wear the grey

A light-horseman takes a sniping shot over a trench parapet on Gallipoli. Snipers often worked in pairs, an observer with a periscope first establishing the target and the sniper rising quickly to fire at it.

flannel shirt with a field dressing sewn inside it and a square of white calico on the back for identification in the dim light. Some wore breeches, some their shorts. Sun helmets were specified, but some men retained their trusty slouch hats. In chilling detail, rifles were to be carried "unloaded and uncharged", with fixed bayonets, a device adopted by both sides as an encouragement for men to keep running until they hit the enemy trenches. Steps were cut in the forward wall of the trench and pegs driven in at shoulder height to aid the hop-over.

On the evening of August 6, many of the lighthorsemen at Russell's Top could see the infantry attack on Lone Pine far down to the right. A sleepless night of battle passed; then, as dawn came, the regiments stood to, awaiting the artillery bombardment of the formidable Turkish positions only 50 metres away.

At about 4 a.m. a destroyer steamed inshore and opened fire with a single gun in the direction of the Nek. The shells fell well past the Turkish front line. The bombardment stopped at 4:23, seven minutes early – an eternity for the men of the first wave. Turkish reinforcements crammed into the Turkish trenches; they bristled with bayonets, as a countryman put it, "the way a stubble paddock looks like when you've put sheep across it, and they've turned the earth up a bit, and you see the stubble standing in rows behind their tracks."

At 4:30, the first line of the 8th Light Horse Regiment leapt over the parapet, and the waiting Turkish trenches exploded in a blizzard of rifle fire and crossfire from an estimated 30 machine-guns. Breathless watchers tried to register what was happening and later tried to convey what they had seen. From Pope's, down to the right, one man watched the first wave running across the skyline suddenly grow limp and fall "as though the men's limbs had become string." Another said, "They fell in heaps. It almost looked as if they had thrown themselves prone to get cover." Perhaps the most remarkable image came from a waiting officer of the 10th: "The air was hazy with lead."

From the first line, an officer and three men reached the Turkish trenches, pinned helplessly below the parapet. One man of that four would survive. The second line of the 8th scrambled over the dead and wounded into the renewed hailstorm of lead. Three or four reached the Turkish trench before they died. In three minutes, more than half the 8th Regiment were dead, and another 80 were wounded.

Cancellation of the attack was proposed and refused by Antill, the brigade major, who had taken over effective command of the brigade from the ineffective and often-sick Colonel Hughes. So now it was the turn of the 10th Regiment. In the words of C.E.W. Bean, the official war correspondent with the AIF, "Mate having said goodbye to mate, the third line took up its position on the firing step." Clive Newman, a 19-year-old trooper of the waiting 9th Regiment, recalled; "One of the 10th Light Horse Officers, a young fellow, turned round before the third line went over and said, 'Well chaps, we've just got ten minutes to live.' " To a whistle blast, the first wave of the 10th now leapt up into the storm of fire. A wounded officer of the 8th, sheltering out on the Nek behind a body, saw the last two men of the line go past, "running in splendid style." A dozen yards on, they "seemed to trip and fall headlong."

Again, cancellation was urged. But before a decision was made, the right flank of the fourth line charged, through some misunderstanding, and the rest of the line followed. Three men reached the Turkish parapet. One of them, Sergeant Sanderson, thought the other two, killed side by side, were brothers Gresley and Wilfred Harper. When Sanderson crawled back to the Australian trenches, he found that "about fifty yards of the line had not a man in it except the dead and wounded." Young Trooper Newman, who was to have gone over with the next wave, looked over the parapet with his periscope but could see only bodies, piled five deep. Of 600 men who had tried to charge across the Nek, 372 were dead or wounded.

The charge at the Nek was one of the tragedies of Australian military history and overshadowed two other Light Horse charges made

George Lambert's oil painting of the charge at the Nek dramatically re-creates the scene of the 3rd Light Horse Brigade's heroic charge to almost certain death.

at the same time – one from Pope's Hill, a little way down to the right of the Nek, and the other from Quinn's Post, further along the rim of Monash Valley. At 4:30, as the horror of the Nek began, 200 men of the 1st Light Horse Regiment charged from Pope's towards four tiers of Turkish trenches. They took three lines of trenches with the bayonet then clung desperately to their position and waged a losing bomb fight with the Turks. When they retired after two hours, only 46 of the 200 were unwounded. The men of the 2nd Regiment at Quinn's Post faced a worse prospect. Here, no man's land was alarmingly narrow – the width of a road in places. At 4:30, the first wave of 55 men charged into the crossfire of four machine-guns and massed rifle fire. Before they could run six paces, 50 of them were dead or wounded. Cancellation of the attack was proposed, and it was confirmed by Chauvel.

Of 255 men who charged from Pope's and Quinn's, 204 were casualties, bringing total losses for the three charges to 576. Allotting blame for these casualties seemed pointless to the men of Anzac. But one thing is certain. If Chauvel or Ryrie had commanded the 3rd Light Horse Brigade that day, the attack on the Nek would have been cancelled when the first wave was cut down.

The attack on Chunuk Bair failed, and the debacle of the British landing at Suvla Bay was a crowning detail of the failed August offensive. Lieutenant Oliver Hogue again captured the mood of Anzac: "Pessimism peeped into the trenches. Later, in the solitude of the dug-out, pessimism stayed an unwelcome guest and would not be banished. All the glorious optimism of April, the confidence of May, June and July had gone, and the dogged determination of August, September and October was fast petering out."

Winter came and the first blizzard, "cold as a Monaro gale." Men warmed their hands by firing five rounds rapid and gripping the barrel of their rifle. Then came rumours of evacuation. The Anzacs were indignant. But they had no say in the matter. The decision that should have been made on April 25 was at last made, seven long months late.

Anzac was evacuated. In a display of logistical and tactical genius – the first of the entire campaign – an army of 41,000 was evacuated by night, without the Turks suspecting anything amiss. On the dawn of December 20, they launched a massive attack to find only empty trenches and 10,000 graves. Ryrie's 2nd Brigade had been among the last men to leave. Both Ryrie and the Light Horse were no longer unknown quantities. The "raw brigades" had proved themselves.

SADDLING UP
FOR WAR

Patiently lined up, recruits wait to be issued with horses and kit at Broadmeadows camp, outside Melbourne.

"I want to shoot the damned Germans, not bite them to death!"

Enlisted light-horsemen examine a doubtful volunteer. At first, only the best physical specimens were accepted in the Australian Imperial Force.

MEN AND HORSES VOLUNTEER

At the outset of World War I, when volunteers could join the branch of service of their choice, men rushed to enlist in the Light Horse. Many rode in from country towns and isolated farms to enlist with their horses; others caught trams in from city suburbs, for the romance of the saddle appealed alike to city dwellers and country men.

Volunteers had to pass a riding test which varied from place to place. In Broadmeadows Camp, Melbourne, they had to ride an army horse bareback and take it over a chock-and-log fence. At Sydney's Rosebery Park, would-be recruits had to negotiate a water jump and a sod wall. A Light Horse officer described how a lad at the Claremont Showgrounds, near Perth, clambered into the saddle from the wrong side and was immediately thrown. He remounted twice and was thrown twice. Eventually he confessed that he had never ridden in his life but was hell-bent on joining the Light Horse. The captain supervising the test told him to practise for a week and come back. The youth returned – and passed.

After they had negotiated the riding test, successful recruits were given a medical – more strict in some places than in others. When a Victorian was rejected because he had false teeth, he protested, "I want to shoot the damned Germans, not bite them to death." He jumped on his motor bike, rode to another town, and was accepted.

Much was made of the patriotism of those early recruits. But one man commented: "Looking back, I'm not sure whether patriotism or the spirit of adventure predominated." Little matter. The Department of Defence showed no uncertainty as it described "the wild, boisterous spirits of the early days eager for adventure." It was all a great romp for the recruits. Their only fear was that the war would end before they could see action.

Volunteers sign on at the Melbourne Town Hall recruiting office. Private soldiers serving overseas were paid six shillings a day, which gave rise to the epithet "six-bob-a day tourists."

Recruits parade in boots and greatcoats for a final medical inspection. Army requirements called for men aged 18 to 35 years, at least 168 centimetres tall, and with a chest expansion of 86 centimetres.

With his protective sun hat still in place, an officer trainee leaps over a vaulting horse in the grounds of the Royal Military College, Duntroon, while (below) burly Light Horse troopers join in a tug of war at Broadmeadows camp near Melbourne.

Dressed in their newly acquired uniforms — with some ill-fitting greatcoats and hats — recruits wait for orders in a bare hut at Broadmeadows. Despite the cheerless appearance, early recruiting camps were the scene of enthusiasm and high spirits.

Men and horses had to learn the discipline of military life before they could take their place in the Light Horse: top, a trooper takes a tumble from his lively mount; centre, a more assured rider holds his seat on a bucking horse; and, bottom, a light-horseman in full kit sits smartly astride his well-mannered waler.

Kitted up and riding four abreast, light-horsemen near the completion of their training at Broadmeadows.

Riflemen stretch out and relax in between sessions of rifle shooting practice at Long Bay (above) and Moore Park (below) in Sydney.

With 43-centimetre bayonet attached to his Lee-Enfield .303 rifle, a trainee takes aim during musketry practice at Long Bay rifle range in Sydney. The Lee-Enfield was the standard small arm for the Australian soldier in both world wars.

Sydney citizens line College Street, Sydney, to farewell members of the 1st Australian Light Horse Brigade as they pass Hyde Park on their way to embark for service overseas. Originally destined for England, the first contingent of the AIF was disembarked at Alexandria for training in Egypt.

Departing light-horsemen watch as the last waler is lifted aboard the transport Omrah at Pinkenba, Brisbane, on September 24, 1914. Horses were later transferred from ship to shore by less ceremonious means; the swinging horse shown below is hoisted aloft in a canvas sling with his nosebag dangling.

2 THE DESERT COLUMN

The Light Horse proved themselves at the Battle of Romani and began driving the Turks back across the Sinai into Palestine. Water was a key strength in defence, a key problem in attack. But problems of command doomed two attacks on Gaza.

When the venerated Lord Kitchener of Khartoum looked at British defences along the west bank of the Suez Canal, he is supposed to have said to General Maxwell, "Are you defending the Canal, or is the Canal defending you?" Maxwell's reply is not known, but he was a fervent believer in making the most of natural defences. His dictum was 'The desert is our ally and will beat the Turks in the end." And it was true that when the Turks attacked the canal in February 1915, only about 25 men from a force of several thousand managed to cross. Four intrepid survivors eventually surrendered in Cairo in response to newspaper advertisements.

The easy British victory tended to obscure the fact that the Turks had in fact crossed the harsh Sinai, in three separate columns, dragging steel punts and field guns. A year and a half later, another Turkish army, this one numbering 20,000 men supported by heavy artillery, would be ready to strike within 40 kilometres of the canal. But a new British Commander-in-Chief, General Sir Archibald Murray, was already committed to an "offensive defence," preparing to defend Egypt on her border with Palestine. His policy placed the Light Horse in the vanguard of the British force, laying the ground for

"The Last Sentry, Moascar" from George Lambert's sketchbook.

their first great mounted action—and the advance that would drive the Turks from Egypt.

The return of the Anzacs evacuated from Gallipoli reunited the Light Horse with their walers. Now they embarked on further training to resharpen their mounted skills and break in a "generation" of reinforcements whose Light Horse career had been spent in trenches.

Early in 1916, with the infantry leaving Egypt for France, there seemed little joy for the Light Horse in this Egyptian "sideshow." On a single day in May 1916, 900 light-horsemen applied for transfer to the infantry. Only the 13th Regiment and two squadrons of the 4th Regiment would go to France to join "the real war" as divisional cavalry, greatly envied by the men who stayed behind. So anxious were light-horsemen to get to France that some abandoned their walers to enlist in the Cyclist Battalion, led by Major Jack Hindhaugh who had worried about the horses on the transport *Wiltshire*.

Chauvel was offered an infantry division in France, but declined. He remained in Egypt as a major-general, commanding the Anzac Mounted Division—three brigades of Australian Light Horse (the 1st, 2nd and 3rd) and one of New Zealand Mounted Riflemen. Two "unbrigaded" regiments, the 11th Light Horse and the 12th Light Horse, were sometimes available to Chauvel, while the remnants of Dad Forsyth's once-proud 4th Light Horse were scattered in the desert, odd-jobbing for the British army. Forsyth himself had gone to France as an infantry brigadier-general, eventually to be broken physically and perhaps mentally. It was no place for a military romantic.

An obscure action on the fringe of the Sinai had already signalled the desert war to come. Major W.H. Scott of the 9th Light Horse Regiment, a consulting engineer in civil life, led a splendidly executed raid on a Turkish party developing new bores at Jifjafa, a small waterpoint in the central Sinai, used by the main Turkish column the previous year. Major Scott destroyed the bore-sinking equipment and took 32 prisoners back to the canal—including an Austrian fellow engineer; six Turks were killed and Corporal S.F. Monaghan of the 8th Light Horse became the first Australian casualty in the Sinai campaign.

To historian Henry Gullett, Jifjafa was "a pretty, if a slight example of Light Horse work." But it had resounding echoes. To put 90 riflemen and 30 engineers into action, this desert raid had taken 320 officers and men, 175 horses and 261 camels. The massive logistics of conventional desert campaigns were highlighted, the Australian waler performed remarkably well against the camel, and General Murray saw that the Light Horse had what he called "a genius for this desert life." Most importantly, this "pretty" exploit discouraged the Turks from attempting their major route across central Sinai. Taking the alternative coastal route, the Turks would water at El Arish and then face a 95-kilometre march across coastal sand dunes to the bountiful group of oases between Katia and Romani, the area the ancients called "the Step to Egypt," only 40 kilometres from the canal. Clearly, El Arish and Katia were vital to Murray in his defence.

The War Office, obsessed with the Western Front, gave grudging permission for the occupation of Katia. So Murray launched a railway and 30-centimetre water pipeline towards the vital oases under the protection of British Yeomanry cavalry, who established posts at Katia and Oghratina, with a reserve at Romani near the railhead.

On April 22, aerial reconnaissance reported a Turkish advance towards the oases. The British took no timely action. But Chauvel ordered Ryrie and the 2nd Light Horse Brigade to Kantara, 24 kilometres from this key area.

In the still pre-dawn of April 23, while a heavy fog drifted from the sea and settled over the oases, a Turkish and Bedouin force of about 5,000 attacked from the smothering darkness, overwhelming the posts at Katia and Oghratina. The Yeomanry abandoned Romani, but some Scottish infantry held out at Dueidar, only 16 kilometres from the canal. Ryrie and the 2nd Brigade raced to the scene in time for their advance guard to help the Scots drive off the

Australian troops man the trenches at the Suez Canal following the Turkish attack on February 3, 1915.

THE BRIEF BATTLE FOR THE CANAL

On February 3, 1915 – two days after the second contingent of Australian troops arrived in Egypt – a Turkish force commanded by Djemal Pasha made an attack on the Suez Canal in an attempt to capture or destroy Britain's vital artery to the East and to Australia.

The attack was poorly planned and easily repulsed. The Turkish advance across the Sinai in three widely separated columns had been sighted from the air and bombed. A flotilla of pontoons launched on the canal came under heavy fire and only one reached the western bank. And although the Turks occupied British forward trenches, they were forced out by counter-attacks.

Australian troops were brought in as reinforcements, but they were too late to see action. By evening, the main Turkish force had been driven back into the Sinai, having sustained more than 2,000 casualties; 716 were taken prisoner.

The Turkish attack was a dismal failure, and for the remainder of the war the Suez Canal remained secure in Britain's hands.

A cargo ship steams past the spot on the Suez Canal where the Turks launched their pontoons.

Timbered and sandbagged trenches forming part of the defence works of the canal zigzag along the east bank.

British soldiers stand guard over a group of Turkish prisoners taken during the attack on the canal.

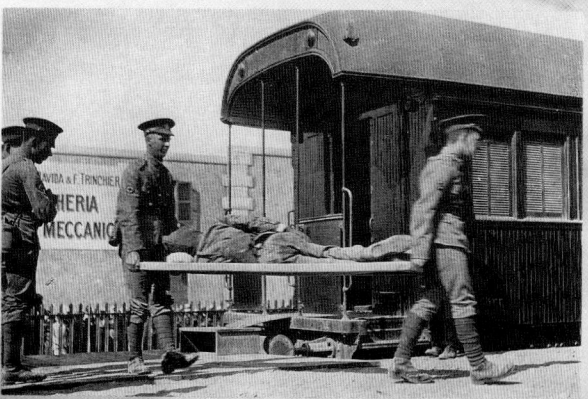

A Turk wounded in the unsuccessful attack on the canal is taken from a hospital train in Cairo.

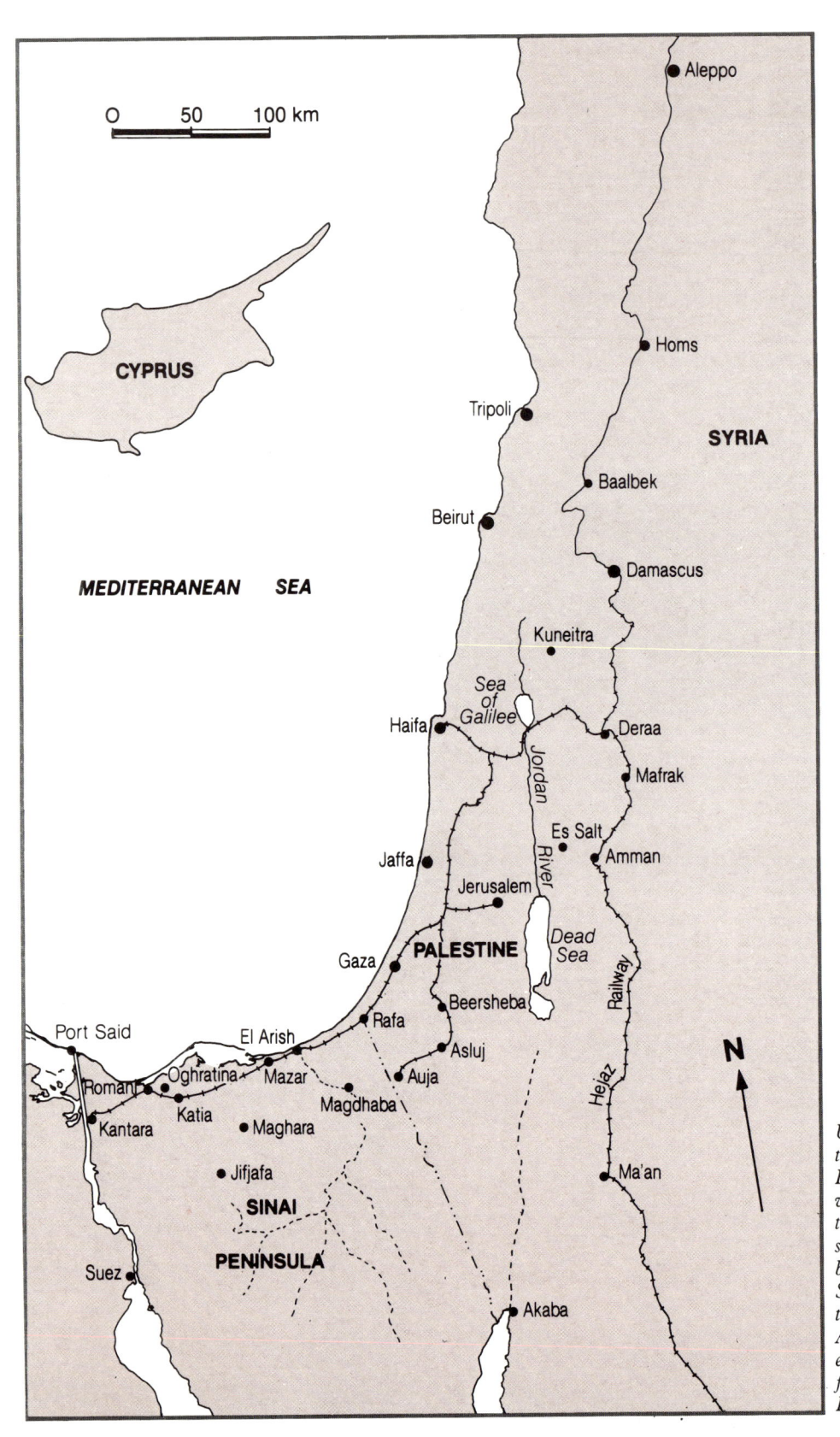

Until early 1916, the task of the British commander in Egypt, General Maxwell, was confined to defending the Suez Canal. Maxwell's successor, General Murray, began the reconquest of the Sinai Peninsula, and with the arrival of General Allenby in June 1917, the expulsion of the Turkish forces continued through Palestine to Damascus.

Turks. At the other posts they found grisly scenes. Some men had been bayoneted as they slept. Some had been strangled with wire. Many of the wounded had been stripped and left to die; others were found wandering in the desert days later. But that was the nature of the war and the enemy. What disgusted the light-horsemen was the apparent fecklessness of the Yeomanry, particularly the officers. Ryrie wrote: "They were not the right people to put at this sort of job," naming five English lords whose luxury foodstuffs, abundant liquor and sporting equipment had been left behind in the scramble to evacuate Romani, even though the Turks had not even approached the camp.

For the rest of the campaign, the Light Horse attitude towards the Yeomanry would swing from contempt to tolerance and eventual respect. Their introduction to the Scots as hardy fighters began a remarkable three years of mutual admiration.

Yet another British officer, Major-General the Honourable H.A. Lawrence, was in charge of this part of Egypt. He placed Chauvel in command of the oasis area with the 2nd Light Horse Brigade and the New Zealanders, while the 1st and 3rd Brigades remained under British command in other sectors. In time, Chauvel would win back his 1st Brigade but lose the New Zealanders. But something went right.

The unattached 12th Light Horse Regiment – still to be issued with their horses – marched to support the Scots at Dueidar, under their new commanding officer, Colonel John R. Royston. Royston was phsically in the Ryrie mould – a 56-year-old weighing more than 100 kilograms. He came from South Africa, but no officer had more experience leading Australian mounted troops in action. He had commanded Australians in the Boer War, formed a basically Australian contingent during the Zulu Rebellion of 1908, and led a predominantly Australian regiment against the Germans in South and West Africa in 1914–15. Apart from this, he was a fearless leader and a recklessly brilliant horseman who scorned military protocol when it stood in the way of effective operation – altogether the perfect man to command light-horsemen. Royston would play a notable role in their first great battle with the Turks.

As the Egyptian summer seared the Sinai with shade temperatures of 50 degrees Celsius (assuming one could find shade), Chauvel sent his men on constant patrol in the Romani-Katia area, brigade by brigade in gruelling 24-hour stretches. After one reconnaissance, 160 men collapsed from heat exhaustion. But the desert skills of the light-horsemen were being further honed, and the terrible dune country became their backyard.

A second sortie into the central Sinai – this time by the 3rd Brigade – had destroyed another 23 million litres of stored water. The central route was now immpossible for the Turks. But Murray, in Cairo, still dithered about giving Chauvel his complete Anzac Mounted Division. So, as reports arrived of a major Turkish advance towards the oases, Chauvel prepared for battle with only two brigades, the 1st and 2nd Australian Light Horse.

Every day now, the Light Horse had minor clashes with Turkish patrols and brought in a steady stream of prisoners. They were now operating on brackish Sinai water treated with chlorine tablets – a one-quart water bottle per day – as the hot summer wind blasted across the dunes and whipped up the kilts of the Highlanders who had marched in as infantry reinforcements.

On June 19, to Chauvel's aggravation, Ryrie took six weeks' leave for parliamentary duties – an Imperial Conference in London. Into this massive gap stepped the equally massive South African, Colonel Royston, now an acting brigadier-general commanding the 2nd Light Horse Brigade. The cast was complete and the stage set for the Turkish strike at the Suez Canal.

The Turkish forces were commanded by the Bavarian Major-General Kress von Kressenstein, a gaunt, aristocratic man, superbly fitted for the chess game of desert warfare. He commanded an enlarged infantry division and a camel regiment, with artillery batteries and machine-gun companies commanded by

Brigadier-General J.R. Royston, commander of the 3rd Light Horse Brigade.

GALLOPING JACK

Young Jack Royston's schoolmates in Durban, South Africa, called him "John Bull." It was a good nickname for a square-built lad of such pure patriotism and martial spirit.

As a teenager, Royston fought in the Zulu War. By the outbreak of the Boer War he was already 39 and a squadron sergeant-major in the Natal Border Rifles; he was immediately commissioned lieutenant and soon distinguised himself at the siege of Ladysmith. A healthy disregard of military protocol was shown during a clash with Boers when he was taken prisoner by a sergeant of the Gordon Highlanders for "interfering with his order of command."

Royston was a captain when given command of the 5th and 6th contingents of the West Australian Mounted Infantry in April 1901. So began what he referred to as "my career as a leader of Australians." He was awarded the CMG and the DSO in the field with them.

When he came to Egypt and joined the 12th Australian Light Horse Regiment as its new commanding officer in 1916, Royston had already commanded Australians in the Boer War, the Zulu Rebellion of 1908 and the campaigns in South and West Africa of 1914–15. He told his first Light Horse parade, "Well, boys, I have been sent to join you and lead you. Treat me right and I'll treat you right." He would later say, "The Australian cannot be driven; but he might be led anywhere."

The men of the Light Horse loved him. They loved his courage, his bull-at-a-gate leadership and his remarkable horsemanship. Royston's aide-de-camp, "specially selected for reckless riding," could not keep up with him on wild cross-country gallops. He would later call Royston "brave, magnificent, spectacular, imposing ... a dashing man, of quick decision, yet so humble, sincere and lovable." A Light Horse legend was in the making.

Germans and Austrians. Von Kress (as he signed himself) issued a document urging his troops "to drive the English into the sea as at Gallipoli."

Major-General Lawrence believed that von Kress would engage the British infantry entrenched across the front of the Romani oases, then attempt to outflank the defences to the south and cut in behind them. He wanted Chauvel to cover this southern flank and fall back in front of the Turkish advance, drawing the enemy into a position where they could be broken by a counter-attack.

On the night of August 2, the Turks occupied the Katia oasis, only 11 kilometres from Romani. With a shrewdness bolstered by good intelligence, Chauvel moved two regiments of the 1st Light Horse Brigade, under Colonel J.B. Meredith, into the southern flank on the following night. They took up a defensive line with their horses well back. As the 2nd Brigade returned from fighting patrol and moved through the 1st Brigade screen to their camp, the Turks advanced behind them from Katia.

Trooper Humphrey Kempe of the 3rd Light Horse Regiment lay in the cool sand with his mates, staring into the darkness. "Used to waiting, we murmured softly to each other," he recalled, " when all at once there before us was our target – the largest body of moving Turks I had ever seen; and far too close. They showed clearly and most menacingly in the brilliant starry night against the white sand as they shouted and screamed, calling on Allah and crying 'Finish Australia', 'Australian finish' with an occasional 'bastard' thrown in for good luck." The Turkish line opened fire and steadily advanced, outnumbering the Australians by nearly ten to one. But the light-horsemen held their ground with their own battle cry: "Allah, you bastards! We'll give you Allah!" Bayonet charges were met with the bayonet and taunts of "Try it again!"

It was now about 1 a.m. Already some Australian posts had been engulfed. Major M. Shanahan of the 2nd Regiment found four of his men who had been cut off and their horses bayoneted. He rode back through the Turks with two men on his horse and two hanging on to his stirrups. As the Turks tried to outflank the Light Horse line on its right, the men steadily moved back, fighting from sand ridge to sand ridge in the dying moonlight. A huge dune dubbed Mount Meredith was a fortress to a tiny garrison of Australians as Turks struggled up its cliff-like face, bootless, fighting for every step in the loose sand, dodging the shot and bayoneted men who rolled down to the base. But by 3. a.m. the enemy was closing in along the easier slopes to both sides, and the handful of defenders abandoned the position.

By now the Australians were being forced back to their horses. They mounted and swung back to a second line of defence, like an opening gate hinged at their left. Some men, boots and leggings clogged with sand, were caught before they could mount; others were double-dinked away by their mates as the Turks closed in. One big Queenslander saw a horseless man and heaved him up on to his horse's rump before he found that he was a Turk; the Queenslander swiftly dumped his unwanted passenger back down onto the sand.

With the first light of dawn on the pale sand, the Light Horse could see the mass of Turks again enveloping their right. They fell back in classic style, squadron by squadron, troop by troop. One troop would hold their ground while another mounted and rode back, halting and wheeling on the order "Sections about – action front!", to dismount and open covering fire as their horses were led back. Under this covering fire, the remaining troops fell back to carry out the same manoeuvre.

The Turkish advance continued forcing the right, and the 1st Brigade made another superb fighting withdrawal, this time riding up the slope of a long dune called Wellington Ridge to take a line along its crest. By now it was full daylight and Chauvel could assess the position. Remarkably unperturbed and completely confident in his 1st Brigade, he had been holding Royston and the 2nd Brigade in reserve. Now he and Royston rode forward at the head of the fresh troops and cantered up to the firing line on Wellington Ridge. It was 4.20 a.m. Two of Royston's regiments raced through a hail of machine-gun fire and shrapnel to reinforce the threatened right, but still the Australian line was forced back, yielding another huge dune, Mount Royston, to the Turks.

Daylight had brought a greater menace from Turkish artillery. But it also meant that the British Territorial Horse Artillery batteries could support the Light Horse defence and drive enemy machine-gunners from the hard-won high points. Nevertheless, by 7 a.m. Chauvel and his brigades had been forced off Wellington Ridge. Yet it was an hour later before the Turks reached the Australian positions on the crest. They were tiring, the sun was climbing higher, the heat was building, and they were 112 kilometres from their water supply at Katia. But the same sun smashed down on the light-horsemen. The 1st Brigade had been fighting for seven hours, the 2nd Brigade had not slept for two nights. The light-horsemen formed a flimsy line protecting their camp, the railhead with its supply dumps, and the vital group of oases.

Now, according to Major-General Lawrence's plan, the Turks would be taken in their exposed left flank. Any moment, Chauvel expected to see the New Zealand Mounted Rifles strike from the south-east. But Major-General E.J. Chaytor, commanding the New Zealanders and the 5th Yeomanry Brigade, was under the orders of Lawrence. And Lawrence was sitting by a useless phone, 40 kilometres away at Kantara on the Suez Canal. The line had been cut. As a result, the New Zealanders, the Yeomanry and the waiting 3rd Brigade started out for Romani late and with confused orders; the 3rd Brigade would not even join the battle that day. However, on their own initiative, a squadron of Yeomanry – the Gloucester Hussars – reinforced Chauvel's threatened right and a battalion of British infantry supported his left. But the Turks, with their superior numbers, kept forcing them back; by afternoon, the light-horsemen had been pushed back so close to their camp that cooks were serving tea to men in the firing line.

Chauvel was riding around the Australian

Right: Troopers leave their horses by a palm hod and advance on foot across the sand in George Lambert's depiction of the Battle of Romani.

positions, keeping in contact with his officers, ignoring enemy fire. He had never been a popular leader, but on this day his calmness and courage won the admiration of his men. Sadly, he was overshadowed by Royston, who had been galloping all over the battlefield since his arrival, booming out encouragement: "Keep your heads down lads. Stick to it, stick to it! You are making history today." A trooper commented, "He was really quite magnificent and I am sure saved us from what might have occurred at any time in those conditions – an ill-advised and distressing retirement to other positions."

As Royston swept past, one man called "Good old Galloping Jack!" And so the Light Horse legend of 'Galloping Jack" Royston was born. The *Official History* says he went through 14 horses that day (Royston himself admitted to only six or eight) and recounts how he galloped up to a threatened group on the right, calling, "We are winning now, they are retreating in hundreds!" One of the light-horsemen said afterwards, "And I poked my head over the top and there were the blighters coming on in their thousands." When a bullet lodged in Royston's calf, he submitted to treatment only when ordered by Chauvel, then galloped off before the dressing was completed, trailing yards of bandage. When someone sugggested that this might be mistaken for a sign of surrender, he tore the bandage off. The bullet remained in his leg until his death.

At last, distant horsemen were sighted on the beleaguered right flank. A 2nd Light Horse officer signalled "Who are you?" The reply came back; "Chaytor." Royston galloped out to brief Chaytor before the New Zealanders, supported by Yeomanry, launched an attack on Mount Royston. By 6 p.m., two battalions of Turks had surrendered. Chauvel sent his weary brigades forward and called up British infantry support. But they did not move until 7 p.m. and were quickly stopped by Turkish fire. Chauvel halted his men. The first day's battle was over.

While firing continued overnight, food, water and ammunition were readily to hand for most of the Anzacs. The carefully controlled withdrawal had placed them in a powerful jumping-off position. By contrast, the tired and thirsty Turks were stretched across the British front, trying to overlap its right. Their water lay out to the British left. They were temptingly vulnerable to counter-attack. But that attack was directed by Lawrence, 40 kilometres away.

At 4 a.m. Lawrence sent in the Anzac Mounted Division as foot troops, with British infantry in support; the 3rd Light Horse Brigade would at last attack from the east, after a day's wandering in a wilderness of sand and tactical indecision. A huge, open line of Anzacs walking across the dunes with fixed bayonets swept the Turks from Wellington Ridge, then charged down its slope with wild yells and shook 1,000 Turks into surrender. The main Turkish force broke and started fleeing to the water at Katia. Now, at 6:30 a.m., Lawrence at last placed Chauvel in command of all mounted troops. But his men were scattered over a wide front as infantry. They were withdrawn, watered and mounted by 10 a.m. British infantry, ordered to the attack at 6:30 a.m., inexplicably did not climb out of their trenches until midday and had advanced a mere three kilometres by nightfall.

The 3rd Brigade had struck to the east and found Turks dug in on a commanding sand ridge at Bir el Hamisah, only six kilometres south of Katia. Superbly supported by the Scots gunners of the Inverness Battery, a squadron of the 9th Light Horse Regiment charged to cover below the ridge while men of the 9th and 10th Regiments outflanked it. A mounted dash by a single troop to within 50 metres of the Turkish positions placed them in a perfect position for a bayonet charge. The 20 dismounted troopers took 425 prisoners. The Turkish left flank at Katia was broken, which posed a crucial threat to their retreat.

At this point, a few Turkish shells fell among the victorious Australians. Brigadier-General Antill, the officer who, from his headquarters dugout, had refused to cancel the charge at the Nek, now ordered his men to fall back three kilometres. A bewildered officer of the 10th

Regiment said the order had been given "for some unknown reason." It could be suspected that Antill panicked. A more charitable explanation is that he was not prepared to risk another bloodbath.

Unsupported by infantry and without the fresh troops of the 3rd Brigade, Chauvel's three tired brigades – the 1st, 2nd and the New Zealanders – had advanced to the Turkish-held Katia oasis by mid-afternoon. Knowing that the battle must be decided by nightfall, Chauvel formed the Anzacs up mounted, with fixed bayonets held like lances, and charged across a naked salt flat towards the eight-kilometre band of date palms marking the Turkish positions – and water. In classic style, they moved from trot to canter and then to a gallop. "A fantastic sight," said Trooper Kempe, "for as far as could be seen from left to right was this fluid line of galloping men numbering at the time upwards of two thousand. The sun flashed occasionally on bayonets, some horses were jumping obstructions, men shouting, cheering, often laughing, so exhilarating was the charging gallop, letting loose their spirits with horses and reins." Trooper Ion Idriess of the 5th Regiment wrote in his diary, "The officers waved revolvers and shouted, a roar of voices rose up and in the mad laughter was shouted wild things and the oasis just rushed towards us."

But the world's most tenacious infantrymen were waiting, in superbly chosen positions. Some light-horsemen crashed through screens of palm fronds into open spaces swept by machine-guns. Others wallowed to a halt in a swamp and sent their horses back as they struggled forward on foot. In near-jungle conditions, the action broke into an awful montage of ambush, sniping, stalking and bayonet fighting. Again in Idriess's words, "The Turk was fighting in a snarling fury over every yard of ground. . . he met you, a replica of the berserk, frightened demon that was in yourself." Yet, even in that hell, the Turk remained a clean fighter. Men carrying wounded mates across open spaces were not fired on. But they ran back to the firing line through a hail of bullets.

As the sun set behind him, Chauvel knew that, while a few of his men had won water, most had empty bottles. He ordered withdrawal to Romani. Many men slept in the saddle as they rode back; in the brief halts, the walers sank to the cool sand. When they reached Romani, some had been 60 hours without water, and under saddle most of that time.

Two days later, 24 kilometres beyond Katia, when the Turks massed a larger rearguard at Bir el Abd, covering their retreat to El Arish, Chauvel again attacked. This time, "Galloping Jack" Royston led the 1st and 2nd Brigades. It was Katia all over again. But now the enemy were in formidable trenches and redoubts, outnumbering the Anzacs two to one, and they launched a series of counter-attacks.

Like many of the Light Horse, Trooper Kempe of the 3rd Regiment had been apprehensive about his fight. In the thick of the battle, he was wounded. He recalled: "As I went to mount I felt a severe thump on my wrist and, thinking someone had kicked me when mounting, started to curse careless companions but soon realised it was a wound." With what Kempe called "rough kindness", a doctor told him "to get to hell out of it" unless he wanted to be captured, which the doctor, his staff and the casualties in their care expected to be at any moment. With other wounded men, Kempe set off on a 32-kilometre ride back to Romani.

As the day dragged on to a bloody sunset, even "Galloping Jack" Royston was forced back, and the New Zealanders alone hung on. Chauvel ordered his men to withdraw. "After riding all night and supplied with only a quart bottle of water apiece, they had fought from daylight to sunset in the heat of a foundry. Tanned as they were, their elbows became blistered from the scalding sand as they gripped their hot rifles."

The failures of Katia and Bir el Abd soured the victory of Romani. Murray blamed Lawrence for his remote leadership. Chauvel blamed Murray for dividing command. But the fact was that, for a loss of only 202 men killed and 928 wounded – most of them Anzacs – the British forces had killed 1,250 Turks, wounded 7,000 and taken 4,000 prisoners. Chauvel was quick to acknowledge "a most masterly rearguard action" by von Kress and his Turks; they had travelled as fast as cavalry, hauling artillery by hand over corduroy tracks of desert brushwood, covered by a rearguard which even the Anzac horsemen could not outflank. Yet they were retreating and for the rest of the war would play a defensive role.

Murray's "offensive defence" became an invasion as he pushed his railway and pipeline towards El Arish, closer to the Palestine border. Meanwhile, he withdrew his headquarters to the Savoy Hotel in Cairo and had Lawrence sent to France. He now appointed Lieutenant-General Sir Charles Dobell, who had won a sound reputation in "native wars", as Commander-in-Chief Eastern Force, which included all troops on the Suez Canal and in the Sinai. In his turn, Dobell formed his mounted troops into the Desert Column, under Lieutenant-General Sir Philip Chetwode, a distinguished British cavalry officer from France. Chauvel and the Light Horse observed these glittering new links in the chain of command and hoped for the best.

In mid-September the Light Horse raided the Turkish post at Mazar, and another attack was made in mid-October on Maghara in the Sinai Hills. Although both these attacks were halted before they could achieve success, they kept the Turks moving back. When the Light Horse and the newly formed Imperial Camel Corps Brigade entered the coastal village of El Arish on December 22, the enemy had pulled out two days before.

In the advance to El Arish, the Light Horse found themselves at last on firm ground. Brigadier-General C. F. Cox of the 1st Brigade said, "The hard going for the horses seemed almost miraculous after the months of sand; and as the shoes of the horses struck fire on the stones of the bed of the wadi, the men laughed with delight. Sinai was behind them." But there was little rest at El Arish. A Turkish force of 2,000 held a post at Magdhaba, only 37 kilometres to the south-east, on the Wadi El Arish. Chetwode immediately ordered Chauvel to remove this threat. On the night of their arrival at El Arish, the Desert Column, less the 2nd Brigade, set out, riding all night to be in sight of the Turkish settlement by first light.

Smoke from Turkish campfires hung low in the chilly dawn as Chauvel personally reconnoitred the position from surrounding ridges. Five brilliantly sited and hidden redoubts were grouped on a forbidding plain, among the windings of the eroded wadi bed, one of them virtually a fortified island with a dry moat. Chauvel waited for aerial support and chuckled when the first plane, which came under heavy fire – revealing the positions of the redoubts – dropped a message, "The bastards are there, alright!" He sent his brigades in a wide net around the post, men and horses ghost-like under a coat of chalky white dust. The 3rd Brigade swung to the north and linked with the

General Chauvel, escorted by a squadron of the 2nd Light Horse Regiment, leads a formal march through the streets of Damascus on October 2, 1918, the day after its capture.

Lieutenant-General Sir Harry Chauvel, commander of the Desert Mounted Corps.

HARRY'S HEROES

As a boy on the Clarence River in New South Wales, Harry Chauvel had two heroes – Saladin and Jeb Stuart. Both were legendary leaders of cavalry. When Saladin led the armies of Islam against the Crusaders, his forces repeatedly fell back across the desert to draw the Europeans into overstretched advances, then wheeled and struck at the tired and isolated Christian knights. In the American Civil War, the Confederate cavalry leader J.E.B. Stuart won fame with his long-distance raids behind the Union lines – once with 12,000 horsemen, and on another occasion leading 1,800 men in a swoop across the Potomac to travel 130 kilometres in 27 hours.

Perhaps it was mere coincidence that Harry Chauvel gained Britain's first major land victory of World War I with a dazzling display of Saladin's classic tactic and that in the final Palestine offensive of 1918 his cavalry circled behind the Turkish lines to isolate two armies, travelling 640 kilometres in 12 days. Whether coincidence or not, Chauvel honoured his great cavalry drive by referring to it as his "Jeb Stuart ride."

Chauvel had been associated with horses from infancy. He began his military career in 1886 as a second lieutenant in the Upper Clarence Light Horse, raised by his father the previous year. In 1896 he joined the Queensland permanent military forces and three years later went to the Boer War as adjutant to the first Queensland contingent, rising to command a mounted infantry battalion and the 7th Commonwealth Light Horse Regiment. At the outbreak of World War I he was offered the command of the 1st Australian Light Horse Brigade; three years later he was in command of the largest body of cavalry employed in modern times.

Despite his brilliance as a commander, Chauvel was never an arresting, picturesque figure. As historian Henry Gullett observed, his success lay in his "far-seeing and perfect preparation and exact execution rather than by inspired flashes of genius."

Reserved and aloof in manner, Chauvel was not one to mix with his soldiers as Allenby did. "Great leader as he became," said Gullett, "he missed by his instinctive reserve the satisfaction of becoming a soldier's idol." Chauvel may have followed in the footsteps of his heroes Saladin and Stuart, but he never became a hero to his own men.

ROUGH-AND-READY CAMELEERS

There is something comical about camels. They smell, they make strange noises, they look bemused, they move in a lolloping slow motion that turns the stomach. But in the desert warfare of Sinai and Palestine, they were formidable.

Bearing loads of 160 kilograms, they could go for six days without water and, in sand, travel faster than a horse. A man on a camel could carry five days' water and rations, together with as much camping gear as a resourceful Australian soldier could acquire. And when wheeled transport was useless, as in the Judaean Hills after the driving rain turned the ground into greasy mud, camels climbed the steepest tracks and doggedly transported their heavy loads to the firing line.

The Australian Camel Corps was formed in 1916 to help fight a revolt by the Senussi Arabs in Egypt's Western Desert; it was based on four companies of infantry just back from Gallipoli. A battalion of English and Scots transformed the unit into the Imperial Camel Corps, eventually enlarged by a battalion of Anzacs and another of Australians. Full strength of the brigade was about 2,800, with the capacity of putting into the firing line 1,800 rifles, 36 Lewis guns, eight Maxim guns and six nine-pounders.

Australians of the Imperial Camel Corps line up on the sandhills near Rafa.

The cameleers were a tough lot, a high proportion of the Australians being problem soldiers happily unloaded by infantry battalions. But they proved magnificent fighters. An eyewitness recalled dismounted cameleers charging the Turkish trenches at Rafa "laughing, smoking and jesting." At Mussalabeh, when a company of cameleers defending the small rocky plateau ran out of bombs to throw, they heaved rocks onto the Turks below and won Allenby's congratulations for their coolness against fearful odds. Mussalabeh came to be known as the Camel's Hump.

Major Oliver Hogue, a former Light Horse officer, commented: "None of us really liked our camels. Frankly, most of us loathed them." Yet when it came time to give up his camel, he would write:

So it's farewell now, old Hoosta,
our paths diverge from here,
I have got to be a horseman now,
and not a cameleer.
You were smelful, you were ugly.
Now I've got a horse instead.
Still you had the camel virtues,
so I'll take back all I said.

New Zealanders. The 1st Brigade and the Camel Corps would strike from the north-west and west. The first moves forward drew heavy Turkish fire from the Turkish redoubts.

In the attack, Royston was commanding the 3rd Brigade. When the acting commanding officer of the 10th Regiment was wounded, Royston appointed 22-year-old Major Horace Robertson in his place. On an aerial report that Turks were retreating to the east, Robertson led the regiment in a wide sweep eastwards and galloped down on 300 startled Turks who surrendered without a fight. A senior officer, about to give up his sword, could not believe that the youthful Robertson, dusty and unshaven like his men, was in command. Assured that he was, "the Turk handed over his weapon with the air of a man resigned to a violent death at the hands of savages."

After a rapid mounted advance through the sandy ridges, Chauvel's men were making slow progress across the more open country, on foot, under heavy fire. Magdhaba on its wadi plain shimmered in a noonday mirage. Chauvel had written of the victory at Romani, "It was the empty Turkish water bottles that won the battle." Now, it was his light-horsemen whose water bottles were emptying. And their walers were 37 kilometres from water unless the Magdhaba wells were taken.

In early afternoon, Chauvel signalled Chetwode that he advised breaking off the attack. At the same time, he ordered his brigade commanders to withdraw. General Cox of the 1st Brigade was about to launch a bayonet charge when the signal reached him. In a clear demonstration of how he had earned his nickname, "Fighting Charlie", Cox barked: "Take that damned thing away and let me see it for the first time in half an hour", then sent in his men. They literally raced Australians of the Camel Brigade to a redoubt, and the first Turks surrendered.

At the same time, young Major Horace Robertson formed up the 10th Regiment, dismounted, with fixed bayonets, and charged them at a second redoubt. The Turks surrendered as the charge hit. Royston was credited with this action, but he had actually led another mounted charge, cobbled together from the "pack leaders and odds and ends of men who were supposed to be holding the led horses." Confronting eight Turkish soldiers in a wadi, Royston thrust his riding cane at them and barked in Zulu, "Hands up!" The Turks dropped their rifles and surrendered, to join the 10th Regiment's bag of 722 prisoners.

Suddenly, Chauvel had a victory on his hands. his men poured in on Magdhaba from every quarter and rounded up nearly 1,300 prisoners, including an indignant French military observer who had strayed from Chauvel's headquarters and forgot to speak English. Chauvel had lost only 22 men killed and 124 wounded.

The wells could not cope with the victorious force. Leaving small campfires beside each group of wounded to warm them and guide ambulancemen, the Anzacs headed back to El Arish. For many light-horsemen, this was their fourth night without sleep, and they plodded towards the coast in a cold, dusty dream world. Many men told of riding through exotic townscapes with brilliant light streaming into the darkness from ornate windows, and unearthly creatures slinking off. Even Chauvel and one of his officers broke away to chase an invisible fox. The Desert Column arrived back in El Arish in the dawn of Christmas Eve.

Two weeks later, an almost identical action would offer the same problems and tempt Chetwode into the same mistake almost made by Chauvel at Magdhaba – a premature decision to withdraw. The Turks had retained a garrison of 2,000 at a Palestine border post near Rafa. On the late afternoon of January 8, 1917, Chauvel's men, strengthened by the Yeomanry Brigade, set out on the 48-kilometre ride to attack it – this time under the direct command of Chetwode, who rode with Chauvel. During the night, they came upon grass and let their horses graze – for many of them, the first time since leaving Australia. With the dawn, having passed the Palestine border markers, they viewed a landscape of grass, clover and barley, brilliant with winter wildflowers.

Above: Dismounted light-horsemen of the 9th Regiment move quickly across open country to attack Magdhaba on December 23, 1916. Scarcely any Turks escaped; 97 were killed and about 300 were wounded, while 1,282 were taken prisoner. Below: A group of prisoners stride across the sand following their capture.

Rafa was a daunting sight by early sunlight, an ants' nest of fortifications and alarmed Turks, dominated by El Magruntein, a hill of tiered trenches. But Chetwode set to it with a will — at least at first. In a series of short advances covered by artillery and machine-gun fire, the attackers closed to within 350 metres of the defences. Losses were heavy, however. Trooper Henry Bostock, a 3rd Brigade scout, recalled, "On our right flank the only cover for the attacking troops [was] an old washed-out road, which had been cleverly covered by a German machine-gunner at right angles. This road was full of dead and dying. There were also clumps of rushes here and there and behind every one was a dead man."

By mid-afternoon the attack seemed stalemated, and even Galloping Jack Royston was bluffed. With two scouts now tailing him in case his horse was shot, he made "many mad gallops" along the firing line, according to one of the scouts, and circled the entire position without finding a point for mounted attack.

At about 4 p.m., scouts reported 2,500 Turkish reinforcements approaching. Chetwode suggested breaking off. Chauvel agreed, and the order went out at 4:25 p.m. Chetwode accepted defeat, mounted, and set his horse's head for El Arish. But behind him the New Zealanders to the north and the cameleers to the south were already charging up long, bare slopes towards Turkish redoubts. Covering fire was so heavy that, in Chaytor's words, the northern redoubt was "smoking like a furnace." Yet Turks could still be seen standing to get better aim down the slope. But neither charge faltered and, at the last minute, the Turks surrendered. After the white flag was shown, a German officer ordered a machine-gunner to fire, killing a Camel Brigade officer. The German was captured, court-martialled, and shot by firing squad 11 days later. A similar incident at the other redoubt led to immediate reprisals from the New Zealanders. Trooper Bostock recalled "the Turkish dead lay in heaps."

The Camel Brigade and the New Zealanders had started a general rush. Men were already charging the remaining 11 redoubts, and white flags appeared all over the battered ants' nest of El Magruntein. Chetwode and Chauvel had another victory plucked from defeat, much more costly than Magdhaba, with 71 killed and 415 wounded. But the Turks had lost 200 killed and 1,600 prisoners.

The light-horsemen had entered Palestine. They had mastered the dunes of Sinai and now found themselves in a land remarkably like much of Australia – dry, open country with eroded gullies and rolling hills. Perhaps this helped them complete their evolution as a unique breed of mounted troops. All pretence of British cavalry style had vanished. They rode with a loose grace that carried its own clear message of confidence and authority. One could call it a bush riding style, but it was bush riding with a marked difference. In the bush, men rode as individuals, each man aggressively distinct from those around him. These men rode as individuals with a sense of belonging to a remarkable group, from which all sense of competition had vanished. The impact of the group was formidable, and each man retained something of that power. They had entered the Sinai as men on horseback. Now, they entered Palestine as light-horsemen – men and horse bonded as a living and fighting entity.

A week after Rafa, Chauvel's knighthood was announced. Following Romani, Murray had recommended Chauvel for a decoration which Chauvel considered inadequate and a slur on his men. He was ignored in the New Year Honours, but his knighthood was announced shortly afterwards. No mention was made of Romani, which had been described by Chauvel as "the first decisive victory gained by British land forces." Imperial and personal politics would continue to dog the Australians.

Murray was creating a second mounted division, incorporating a new Australian Light Horse brigade, the 4th, made up of the 11th and 12th Regiments and the re-formed 4th Regiment. With the 3rd Brigade, they would join two Yeomanry brigades as the Imperial Mounted Division. The name galled the Australians, as did the appointment of a British officer to command them, the thoroughly solid Major-General H.W. Hodgson. The remaining brigades of the Anzac Mounted Division, still under Chauvel, would be built up to strength by another Yeomanry brigade. Meanwhile, Murray's ponderous but admirable arteries of war, his pipeline and railway, edged into Palestine as the British forces prepared for their next strike at the Turks.

Von Kress had drawn back to a scattered 48-kilometre line across southern Palestine, between fortress Gaza, on its low plateau near the coast, and the frontier town of Beersheba in the Negev – the drylands between the Sinai and the Dead Sea. Gaza was all but impregnable, flanked by commanding ridges which had been expertly fortified. Dominating them all was the steep, blunt peak of Ali Muntar, up whose slopes Samson was said to have carried the gates of Gaza. The town was surrounded by closely cultivated fields with thick hedges of prickly-pear cactus – often more than 2.5 metres high – which flanked narrow laneways and created a defensive maze in places three kilometres deep.

The attack on Gaza, under General Dobell, was set for March 26. The mounted troops and one infantry division would encircle the town to prevent retreat and cut off reinforcements, while infantry made a direct assault on the key fortress of Ali Muntar. A secondary role of the horsemen would be to support the infantry attack. It was a sound enough battle plan, but the command structure was too divided. Murray was in overall command, Dobell would direct the attack, while Chetwode commanded the attacking infantry, who were under another officer, Major-General G.A. Dallas. Dobell retained command of the remaining infantry, who would form part of the cordon

The Light Horse advance towards the outskirts of Gaza. With victory within their grasp, the attacking force was withdrawn because of a prearranged plan to call off the attack if it had not succeeded by sunset.

and also be in reserve for the attack. The division of command, compounded by poor communication, would doom the action.

The Light Horse sent out reconnaissance in force. On March 23, three days before the attack, Royston's 3rd Brigade inspected the defences and captured three Turkish officers. When it was suggested that the Turks might withdraw in the face of the huge British attack, "one of them smiled, and politely touching his fez, replied, 'Pardon, sir, I do not think so. We gave you Rafa, but we will not give you that,' pointing towards Ali Muntar."

At 2:30 a.m. on March 26, the Anzacs led the Imperial Mounted Division in the wide, looping movement to cut off the town. By dawn, a dense fog had rolled in from the sea. The lighthorsemen welcomed it as a screen for their movement, using luminous prismatic compasses set in glycerine which enabled readings to be taken from horseback. The infantry were slightly delayed by the fog. Soon after sunrise the fog lifted, and by 10 a.m. the Anzacs had circled right around to the coast north of the town and captured a Turkish general on the way. An excited dispatch rider reported to the Imperial Mounted Division, further to the east, "We've taken Gaza and captured the boss of the whole outfit." He was wrong on both counts but accurately expressed the enthusiasm of the Anzacs. During the morning, water was found for two complete brigades, while individual troops and sections filled buckets for their horses from communal wells.

Meanwhile, within the 24-kilometre cordon of mounted troops, a tragic farce was being played. Chetwode, deterred by the fog, decided against a forward headquarters and set up beside Dobell, five kilometres back. The fog had cleared by 8 a.m., and within half an hour the infantry were on their start line for the attack on Ali Muntar. But their commander, Major-General Dallas, was not ready. He waited until 9 a.m. to gather his commanders for a briefing, which eventually started at 10:15 a.m. He issued orders for the attack at 11 a.m., informing a surprisingly tolerant Chetwode that, owing to a delay in placing artillery, his troops would not be ready to advance until noon. He did not seem to know that his guns had been trained on Ali Muntar for the past hour.

Dallas began his bombardment at noon – only after an impatient order by Chetwode – and the infantry, who had been waiting for three and a half hours, at last moved forward. Even though the bombardment was falling uselessly on a cemetery behind Ali Muntar, the troops advanced with dogged courage against heavy artillery fire and soon were fighting Turkish infantry in a cactus maze dubbed the Labyrinth.

Frustrated by Dallas's immobility and this late start, Chetwode signalled Chauvel at 1 p.m. to throw the Anzac Mounted Division against Gaza. But Chauvel did not receive the order until 2 p.m. and could not gather his horsemen for the attack until 4 p.m. Then they dashed forward, led by the 2nd Brigade on the right, with New Zealanders and Yeomanry to the left.

The 5th Light Horse Regiment were galloping across a field of olive trees when they came on a tangle of prickly-pear hedges. The men reined to a plunging halt and dismounted. Trooper Idriess wrote, "All along the hedge from tiny holes were squirting rifle-puffs, in other places the pear was spitting at us as the Turks standing behind simply fired through the juicy leaves.

The horse-holders grabbed the horses while each man slashed with his bayonet to cut a hole through those cactus walls. . . It was just berserk slaughter. . . the Turkish battalion simply melted away: it was all over in minutes." An officer was surprised to see an old sergeant firing over a cactus hedge from the saddle while his horse nibbled at the grass. Asked why he did not dismount, the sergeant replied, in between shots, "I can see them better from here."

A squadron of the 5th Regiment and New Zealanders smashed through successive cactus walls and captured two field guns. When they came under fire from Turkish machine-gunners in a stone house 70 metres away, the New Zealanders swung one of the captured guns, opened the breech block, sighted down the barrel, then loaded and fired. Two shells crashed through the house, and 28 Turks surrendered. In a shambles of street fighting, the Anzacs shot and hacked their way towards the Great Mosque in the centre of Gaza.

Since 9 a.m. Light Horse patrols had been aware of Turkish reinforcements approaching. Von Kress was uncomfortably aware that his relief troops were, as he later wrote, "poorly trained and equipped" and moving "slowly and cautiously." An officer riding with a column from Beersheba reported that it was led by a Lieutenant-Colonel Edib Bey, "who would have done better as an opera singer than a staff officer" and who slowed his column to three kilometres per hour, "fearful no doubt lest a crisis reveal that his military reputation had no more solid foundation than bluff."

Late in the afternoon, a force of 6,000 infantry advancing from the east were engaged by Royston and the 3rd Brigade. An officer of the 10th Light Horse Regiment reported, "They appeared very tired" and noted that, under long-range fire, "the Turks, apparently nonplussed, deployed and halted." To their right, Yeomanry held further advances, although one brigade was driven back slightly until supported by Royston. News of these clashes reached Dobell and Chetwode in their headquarters, and they nourished each other's concern.

Meanwhile, the British infantry were winning the forward slopes of Ali Muntar with a magnificent series of bayonet charges, while New Zealanders charged its rear positions. It was 6 p.m. and the sun was setting. In Gaza, Major Tiller, chief of staff to the Turkish commander, had reported by wireless to von Kress that he could not hold out until the first reinforcements reached him by dawn. The civic head of the town was preparing a feast to welcome the British conquerors.

At 6.10 p.m., to the astonishment of the apparently victorious infantry and Light Horse, Chetwode, with Dobell's approval, signalled Chauvel to break off the attack and withdraw. The near-disastrous errors of Magdhaba and Rafa had been repeated. "But we have Gaza!" Chauvel protested. When Dobell himself reiterated the order, Chauvel passed it on. Chaytor demanded the order in writing before he would move. Brigadier-General C.L. Smith, commander of the Camel Brigade, sent back a message questioning its authenticity. To a chorus of "What!" from his commanders, Royston demanded that the order be repeated. Ryrie "swore like a trooper" and then refused to budge until every man, living or dead, had been collected.

At 6:30 p.m., as Dallas's infantry finally won the crest of Ali Muntar to the cheers of the Anzacs, the confirmations were still going out: "Retire! Retire! Retire!" Dazed, the Anzacs withdrew from Gaza, one of the sorriest movements undertaken by Australians and New Zealanders during the war.

A Turkish officer reported: "Of the 79th and 125th Regiments of the line that had formed the nucleus of the garrison of Gaza, a mere handful survived." He said that most of the Austrian gun crews were dead, concluding, "The only troops that suffered no losses that day were our Arab volunteers who did not so much as come within range of the enemy's artillery, but waited tranquilly until nightfall to go about slaying the *inglis* wounded and despoiling their bodies of clothing which would be sold later in the adjacent camps and villages."

As dawn broke, both the Turks and the British

realised what had happened. The Turkish commander, Tala Bey, had been blowing up his wireless station and stores. When told of the British withdrawal, "he laughed for a long time." As soon as Dobell realised the scale of his mistake, he sent Dallas and his exhausted troops in a pathetic attempt to reoccupy Ali Muntar. When this failed, he wrote Murray a report on the previous day's action, in which he claimed, "so far as all ranks of the troops engaged were concerned, it was a brilliant victory."

Encouraged or inspired by Dobell's deception, Murray sent a message to the War Office on March 28 telling how an engagement "east of Gaza with a force of about 20,000 of the enemy" had resulted in between 6,000 and 7,000 Turkish casualties. These figures quadrupled the Turkish forces, almost trebled their casualties, and ignored British losses of nearly 4,000. The truth was so effectively concealed that as late as 1919 a British historian would quote the battle as "a complete victory".

Murray's remarkable fallacy made possible, or perhaps demanded, a second attack on Gaza three weeks later. The British Prime Minister, David Lloyd George, was a staunch "Easterner", and he used this supposed victory to convince his War Cabinet that there was some real potential in the Eastern Front. The recapture of Jersusalem from the heathen Turk would recharge the flagging spirits of the British people. Two days after Murray's remarkable dispatch, the war Office promised reinforcements and encouraged him to continue his Palestine offensive "with a view to the occupation of Jerusalem." Murray approached the second battle of Gaza with new spirit.

But von Kress too was encouraged by his windfall victory, and gained precious reinforcements after the withdrawal of Russia from the Caucasus. With 25,000 troops to deploy, he improved and extended the defence of Gaza itself and built a chain of redoubts along the high road to Beersheba.

Murray's railhead was now only eight kilometres from the Wadi Gaza base of Eastern Force. Heavier siege guns arrived by train and were dragged to the front by caterpillar tractors. When a Light Horse officer watched confident British artillerymen selecting positions from which they could "blow Ali Muntar into the sea," he commented, "That hill reminds me very much of Achi Baba at Gallipoli. I remember Achi Baba was to be blown into the sea many times, but it always seemed to bob up again".

More and more, as they studied the dominant, carefully spaced Turkish redoubts with overlapping fields of fire to sweep the naked slopes below them, the coming battle reminded the light-horsemen of Gallipoli. The British infantry would launch a massive attack on a front of some eight kilometres, while the Desert Column struck eastwards on a 10-kilometre front to prevent reinforcements being sent to Gaza. Dobell was stretching his resources to breaking point over 18 kilometres. But he had two surprises: 2,000 gas shells, to be used for the first time on this front, and what one Light Horse officer cynically called "the Crowning Joy of the Army, the Hope of the Side, the mysterious, much-advertised, irresistible, war-winning *Tank*." There was another new weapon as well: the Hotchkiss portable machine-gun, issued one per troop, 12 per regiment. This deadly weapon fired strips of .303 ammunition at rate of up to

The four members of a Hotchkiss machine-gun team look on while a resourceful trooper displays a tripod he improvised from wire-entanglement posts. The tripod enabled the weapon to be used as an anti-aircraft gun.

500 rounds per minute and went into action with a crew of four, including one man to fire the 40-kilogram gun, a feeder for the ammunition, and two men to handle gun and ammunition pack horses.

The second round of the battle for Gaza began on April 17 with a touch of gloves. British infantry advanced and dug in. The Desert Column moved out, located the enemy, exchanged a few shots, and watered their horses. The next day, the Light Horse again probed the Turkish line, with scouts riding out to draw fire and locate enemy positions. One wrote in his diary, "We held a small hill and had some good shooting, but, when returning after dark, were fired on by our own outposts." A Light Horse officer recalled these two days and the nagging question "Why the delay?" and the answers: "Wait till the guns open up on Gaza in earnest! Wait till the tanks. . ." The horses grazed in barley fields; the men prowled.

At 5:30 a.m. on April 19, three warships and massed artillery began to pound Gaza. But the only major success of the entire bombardment was an accidental hit on the Great Mosque, which, fortunately, was being used as an ammunition store. The gas shells proved useless in the high temperatures and coastal wind. Then the six tanks clanked forward at six kilometres an hour and the infantry followed in the main assault on the Labyrinth and Ali Muntar.

To the right, the light-horsemen of the Imperial Mounted Division attacked, leaving their horses in wadis and moving forward under whatever cover was available – often growing barley crops little more than 30 centimetres high, with machine-gun fire scything the stems just above their heads and shrapnel blasting down on their prone bodies. An officer reported: 'There was constant slaughter among the barley. Our fellows took the heavy casualties almost as a joke. 'Stretcher bearers here,' shouted a trooper, 'I've got one in the leg.' He sat up laughing, and was instantly killed by shrapnel."

On the left, closer to the infantry advance, light-horsemen of the new 4th Brigade watched the Tommies on their left walking up a slope behind the tanks, smothered in shell bursts. But they had their own worries. Said one trooper: "I wondered how anyone could walk through

One of the six tanks brought out from England lies disabled after the second battle of Gaza.

machine-gun bullets and shrapnel that seemed to fill the air all the time as we advanced towards the Turkish line. Our troop officer walked along calmly and the mates of our troop didn't look frightened, but they might have felt as scared as I did. The words 'Stretcher bearers!' were heard quite often."

One tank, "The Nutty," commanded by "a dapper little 2nd Lieut." as an Australian officer recalled him, lumbered ahead of the cameleers to take a Turkish redoubt, then, struck by several shells, advanced on a second. Trooper Ion Idriess of the 5th Light Horse Regiment watched, appalled, as the tank "clanked straight for the redoubt. The Australians and Tommies fixed bayonets and charged screaming through clouds of smoke. The tank rolled on with her shell-pierced machinery grating and shrieking, fumes sizzling out from the shell holes in her sides. It was a terrible charge. In the last few yards the struggling monster grew red-hot and belched dense clouds of smoke . . . until in the very centre of the redoubt it burst into flames." With the "dapper little 2nd Lieut." and his crew, almost two companies of Australian cameleers and the Tommies were wiped out.

Trooper J.E. ("Chook") Fowler of the 12th Light Horse described how his regiment was approaching a ridge when they saw a mound of earth with a pole sticking out on top. "We soon knew it to be a 'key' range for Turkish gunners as immediately eight guns opened up with shrapnel." When the smoke and dust cleared, three men remained from a troop of 20. Other groups of men started to dig frantically for cover with their bayonets in the hard-baked clay, said Fowler, dodging the nose caps of shells "speeding along the hard surface of the ground like a cricket ball hit at terrific speed." As they dug, a lookout was posted to warn of machine-gun fire raking across the slope towards them.

To their right, the 3rd Brigade had walked into a similar trap. B Squadron of the 10th Regiment was pinned down in front of a major redoubt when Lieutenant Hugo Throssell, who had won the Victoria Cross at Gallipoli, told a sergeant to order his troops to fix bayonets and charge over about 270 metres. The sergeant responded by telling him "not to be so bloody foolish," and the troops stayed where they were. The regiment had already lost almost half its men from the firing line. Helplessly, men of the 3rd Brigade watched 2,000 to 3,000 Turkish reinforcements from Beersheba reach the redoubt. This was serious. But more serious was the realisation that these troops were not needed at Gaza, where the entrenched Turkish forces were apparently holding their own. Then, in early afternoon, the brigade was reinforced by New Zealanders and Yeomanry for a large-scale bayonet charge. The survivors of the charge at the Nek prepared for another massacre. But Royston called off the attack and ordered his men to fall back. The 10th Regiment had only 35 men in the firing line when it withdrew.

That night, the Light Horse abandoned the few positions they had captured. To the right, the Anzacs had driven back a few demonstrations by large forces of Turkish cavalry and cameleers but gained no ground. To the left, after a day of heroic but suicidal effort, the British infantry held nothing but the jumping-off line they had occupied two days before.

The bombardment had failed, the gas had failed, the tanks had failed, the tactics had failed. And men, asked to do the impossible, had been given no chance of success. Total British casualties of 6,444, including 1,116 in the Desert Column, were officially posted but never accepted by the Light Horse. Figures of 10,000, 15,000 and even 18,000 were widely quoted and believed by officers and men, leading to claims that April 19 had been Britain's costliest day of the war. In a way, it had been. The Light Horse no longer believed in the high command. Words like *murder* and *death-traps* were commonly used as the light-horsemen joined the infantry in general retirement to the Wadi Gaza, leaving the barley fields below the eastern redoubts and the green corn below Ali Muntar to commemorate this bloody day with new fertility.

SURVIVING
IN THE DESERT

A Light Horse officer looks north towards the sand dune known as Mount Meredith, scene of bitter fighting during the Battle of Romani.

"A genius for this desert life"

A HOT AND THIRSTY CAMPAIGN

For the light-horsemen who carried the war into the Sinai desert in April 1916, the months that followed were a test of endurance and adaptability. The extreme heat, the shortage and quality of the available water, and the sickness borne by flies at insanitary camps — all imposed severe hardships on both men and horses. Said war historian Henry Gullett: "The Sinai force would be in danger of destruction during the summer even if the Turks did not fire a shot."

Within a short while, however, the Light Horse adapted to this desolate land with its harsh demands. They learned to cope with the blazing heat, to conserve their water supplies and to improvise equipment and develop techniques that made life bearable.

Water was an ever-present problem in Sinai. While a man might get by with a litre a day, horses needed 22 litres to keep in good condition. Water could be found below the ground in palm groves, or hods, but it was usually brackish, and bitter when touched by the roots of palm trees. A horse would drink the brackish water only when very thirsty.

Wherever they were, their horses needed regular care. When standing on lines, horses were groomed three times daily, watered twice, led three times, and exercised twice. When on the move, they were ridden for 40 minutes, led for 10 minutes, and rested for 10 minutes each hour.

In Palestine, on the coastal fringe, water was more freely available, the land was fertile and the weather mild. But east of this coastal margin was the rugged central range, and beyond that the dry, dusty, insect-infested Jordan Valley, where the Light Horse were to endure a sweltering summer. They were periodically rested in camps and Jewish villages on the coast, but for the most part they endured the ordeal of the Jordan Valley, as they endured Sinai, with a cheerful spirit of self-preservation.

Hoofprints dot the ridges of a sand dune in northern Sinai typical of those over which the Light Horse rode and fought. Southwards from the coastal dunes were stony plains with prickly bushes banked up with driven sand. The dunes near Romani (below) extended inland about 10 kilometres, creating a natural stronghold about 80 square kilometres in extent covering the track from El Arish to the Suez Canal.

The Hod el Bayud, the most southerly oasis in the desert between the canal at Kantara and El Arish, nestles in the bend of a wadi 10 kilometres south of Bir el Abd. Water was always available at shallow depths in these palm hods.

The 1st Australian Light Horse Brigade camps in the shadows of palm trees at the Hod el Ge'eila, east of Bir el Abd. The brigade made camp here for two weeks before the advance to El Arish.

Pools of water cover the ground at the hod in Belah following the heavy rains in January 1918. The 3rd Australian Light Horse Brigade was camped in the locality during this time, resting after the capture of Jerusalem.

Dust raised by the horses' hooves blankets the Wadi Auja as the 8th Light Horse Regiment take their horses to water at the Auja ford. As well as dust, the tr

...ed severely from excessive heat, flies and mosquitoes in the Jordan Valley.

Rows of tethered horses line one side of the 2nd Light Horse Brigade camp at Romani. Problems of sanitation and the disposal of horse litter — in order to reduce the prevalence of disease-spreading flies — were difficult to overcome in desert camps.

A squadron of the 6th Light Horse Regiment line up with their kit near Shellal. As the summer advanced, troopers acquired additional water bottles, sacks for carrying extra horsefeed, and extra reserves of food and water to carry with them on their missions.

A light-horseman can still raise a smile as he swelters in his bivouac on a hillside in the Jordan Valley during July. At this time, the temperature was 49°C.

"COO-EE"

Here's a "Coo-ee", Sister Billjim,
From a Billjim over-seas,
Where there aint no scented Wattle,
And there aint no Blue-Gum trees.

We're among the wavin' date-palms,
Makin' Jacko Turkey-trot,
And send sincerest Christmas Greetings,
From this Gawd-forsaken spot.

Copyright.

EGYPT   1914.
GALLIPOLI 1915.
SINAI   1916.

PALESTINE
XMAS - 1917

Horses of the Anzac Mounted Division feed from their nosebags during a rest in a valley on the way to Es Salt in April 1918. The ration for a horse on the move was 2.7 kilograms of grain a day. At right, mounts of the 6th Light Horse Regiment rest in desert oases. Horses standing on lines developed the habit of eating sand, head-ropes, head-collars and hair off their neighbours; a mule on the 1st Signal Troop lines was shorn clean one night by the two horses on either side of it.

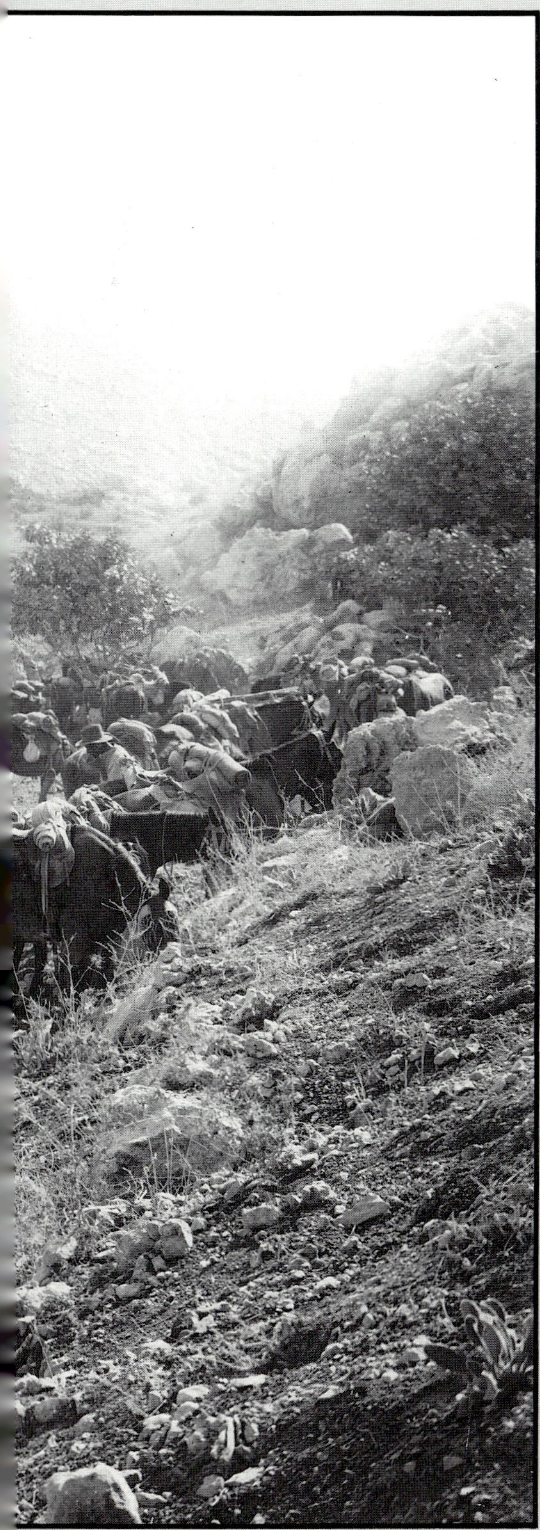

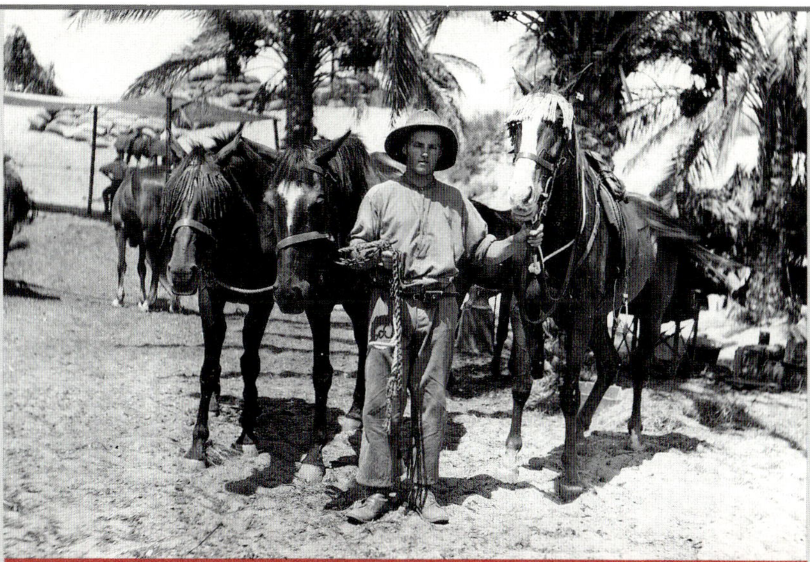

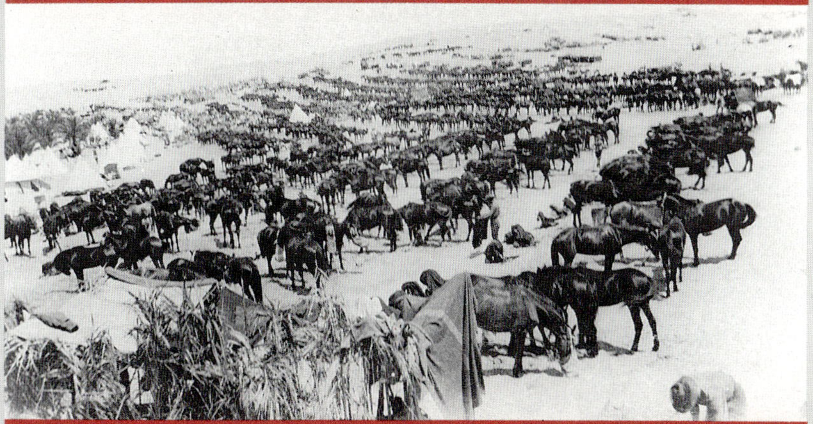

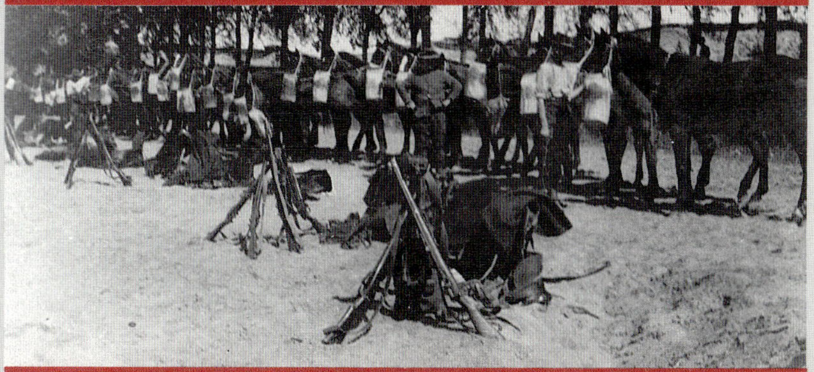

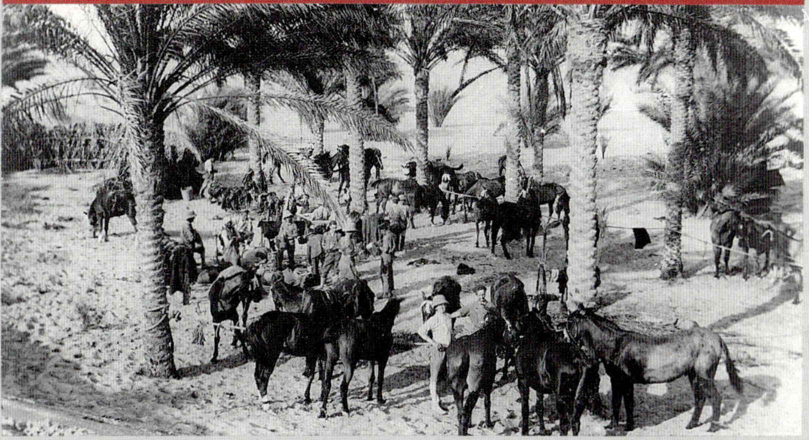

Top: With the band playing in the centre of a sandy ring, light-horsemen join in a game of musical chairs on horseback. Bottom: Eyes lift skywards to watch the spinning coins as these men take part in the less strenuous but more popular pastime of two-up.

FUN AND GAMES IN THE DESERT

It was not all fighting and marching for the men of the Light Horse in Egypt. There were also moments of sport and recreation. The bush balladist Banjo Paterson, who was in charge of a remount unit at Heliopolis, explained in a letter to his publisher, George Robertson, what he arranged to keep the men occupied and amused. "I got the idea of giving a rough-riding display in public," he wrote. "We (my squadron) won five out of seven events open to all troops in Egypt at a show the other day. In the wrestling on horseback, one of my Queenslanders, a big half-caste named Ned Kelly, pulled the English Tommies off their horses like picking apples off a tree.

"You say what does this do towards winning the war? Well, it shows that we are up in our work and are doing it and it is not too easy. At the present moment I have two men with broken legs, one with a fractured shoulder blade, two with badly crushed ankles, and about seven others more or less disabled."

He went on to say, "I have never had to tell a man twice to get on a horse no matter how hostile the animal appeared; in fact, they dearly like to do a bit of 'grandstand' work even though they risk their necks by it."

Horses and men take the strain in a tug-of-war competition on the desert sands.

Bare to the waist and mounted bareback on their walers, tough troopers pit their skill against one another as they wrestle on horseback.

A lucky horse grazes unconcerned and a relaxing trooper looks on while light-horsemen of the Desert Column move off to the Second Battle of Gaza.

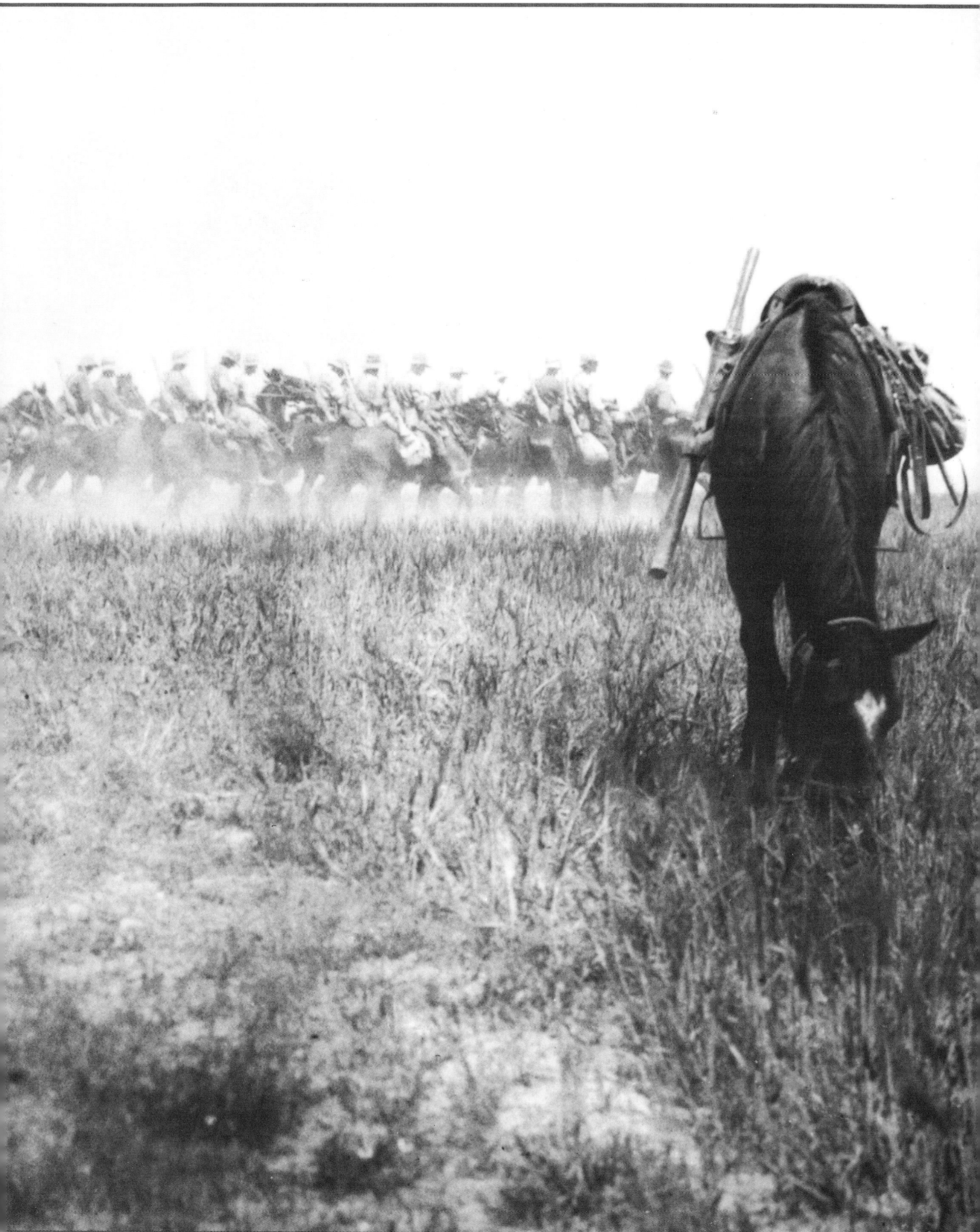

"Their record in this war places them far above the cavalry horses of any other nation"

Troopers of the 9th Light Horse Regiment move along smartly towards Jifjafa, the first engagement of the Light Horse in Sinai, on April 13, 1916. On this march, the waler began to show its superior pace as a walker, an invaluable quality in these campaigns.

Light-horsemen on their sturdy walers stream down the front of a sand dune in Sinai. Some remarkable instances of horses' endurance were recorded; a remount issued to the commanding officer of the 1st Signal Troop in July 1916 carried him more than 11,000 kilometres up to November 1918, an average of 400 kilometres a month, and was in good condition at the end of the period.

With a string headpiece to keep the flies out of the leading horse's eyes, the 7th Sanitary Section of the Light Horse passes along the Wadi Nimrin in Palestine. An enemy machine-gun opened fire near this spot, causing nine casualties out of the full strength of 19.

A light-horseman stops to look at a group of dead artillery horses, casualties of the Battle of Romani. Right: Killed during the same battle, a Red Crescent camel lies amid the tangle of the cacolets it carried to transport wounded soldiers.

Dead horses scatter the sand near an ammunition transport echelon attacked by enemy aircraft during the drive to Beersheba.

The bodies of two Turkish machine-gunners who died at their posts lie beside their silenced weapon.

3

THE CHARGE AT BEERSHEBA

The arrival of General Allenby as Commander-in-Chief and the creation of a new mounted force under Harry Chauvel marked the turning point. Success depended on the capture of Beersheba; Chauvel ordered the Light Horse to charge.

In October 1917, thousands of light-horsemen owed their lives to a little hospital nurse at El Arish with girlish handwriting and a British officer who was studying the birds of Palestine in his spare time. They were key figures in the most remarkable military intelligence coup of the war, which enabled the Light Horse charge at Beersheba to save an army from potential disaster and change the history of the Middle East.

It all started with the dying echoes of the Gaza debacle. While troops were still straggling back across the Wadi Gaza, General Murray sacked Dobell and replaced him with General Chetwode. Chauvel moved up to lead the whole Desert Column — and thus became the first Australian to command a corps. Murray now waged his own rearguard action with the War Office by telegram, blaming his failure on inadequate resources. The War Office back-pedalled on its urgings for a strike at Jerusalem and ordered him simply to take every favourable opportunity of defeating the Turkish forces opposed to him with all the means at his disposal. Then they set about replacing him.

Meanwhile, there were changes in the forces opposing the British. The German Chief of the General Staff, Erich von Falkenhayn, was sent

From the sketchbook of George Lambert.

to oversee the creation of a Turco-German force to recapture Baghdad, which had been taken by the British in March. But victory in Palestine was recognised as a higher priority, and von Falkenhayn hurled himself into the task, trying to hack his way through the resentment of the Turkish high command, who saw Baghdad, home of the caliphs, as a spiritual goal. The resulting delay would prove fatal to both Turkish and German dreams.

While Whitehall, Berlin and Constantinople shaped their destinies, the men of the Light Horse settled into a routine of trench-digging, training, manning outposts by day, listening posts by night, and riding on frequent patrols towards the more open eastern flank. Here, where the country was drier, there was a no man's land of nearly 16 kilometres, and they often sighted parties of Turkish cavalry. An officer noted, "The Turkish horsemen appeared extremely smart and light. Their Arab horses were very sure-footed over rough and broken ground." Another officer was less impressed: "In a party of 20 Turkish cavalry captured by a Light Horse patrol, their horses were so miserably thin one of our men hung his hat on one's rump, thereby greatly annoying the owner." The Turks usually avoided contact or waited until the Australians turned to ride back, then dashed in like terriers to snap a few quick shots at their heels. They tempted some light-horsemen into ambush until the tactic was recognised.

To Galloping Jack Royston, it was like being back on the South African veld. He formed a 3rd Brigade scout unit, nicknamed "Royston's Boys", and took particular interest in its work. One of the scouts, Trooper Harry Bostock of the 10th Regiment, described how they were well out in front one afternoon when Royston and his staff came riding out to join them. "The Turks must have seen them because, soon after, a cavalry troop appeared at the gallop on our extreme right. We pointed this out to the General. 'Yes', he said, 'they are going to try and cut us off. You will cut them off instead.'

"Mounting our horses and at full strength of 30, we rode at the gallop towards their rear. They, in turn, sensed our move and lined a ridge directly in our path. We rode over a bald hill and came right into their rifle fire. The order was 'swing to the right'. I happened to be on the left flank and last over the rise. The bullets were hissing around me when Abdul, my horse, fell on the hard stony ground. I thought he had been killed and had my left leg under him. He had stopped a bullet on the top of his neck just behind his ears but was not hurt really, just enough to drop him. We were both up and gone in quick time. . . .

"The game was now on. . . . Our officer, Lieut. Rickaby, who rode the 'fastest' horse, soon overtook the slowest Turk. He emptied his revolver at him at close range but to no effect. The Turk, being well trained, pulled up his horse and reversed his lance to the rear for Rickaby to gallop into. He nearly did, the lance leaving a rusty mark on his shirt sleeve. The Scout behind, Kincaid (9th Light Horse) dropped the Turk. . . . The running fight continued for some distance – about three miles. We took back five horses and their gear with swords and lances, as proof of our success."

Often, Bedouin scouted for the Turks and fired warning shots when the Light Horse approached. The new boys of the 4th Light Horse Regiment had their first action when, during a search for a large force of Turkish cavalry and camelry, a party of Bedouin ambushed their advance guard, wounding one man and killing one horse. Trooper Malcolm Macdonald wrote to his sister: "I just missed a holiday yesterday, my horse got shot in the stomach. I would have just as soon stopped it as the poor horse. She died afterwards. She carried me about 50 yards out of danger first." The regiment took eight prisoners and neglected to report killing some of the ambushers.

All the time, the light-horsemen were getting to know the country and its vital water points – the wadis where water was close to the surface, the rock cisterns, a few natural, most carved by the Romans, and the Bedouin wells, "the Tears of Allah", some dating back to the days when Abraham and his herdsmen had

Light-horsemen man an outpost on a rocky outcrop on the Philistine plain. The 16 kilometres of no man's land on the eastern flank of the British positions in the Wadi Gaza required continual patrolling.

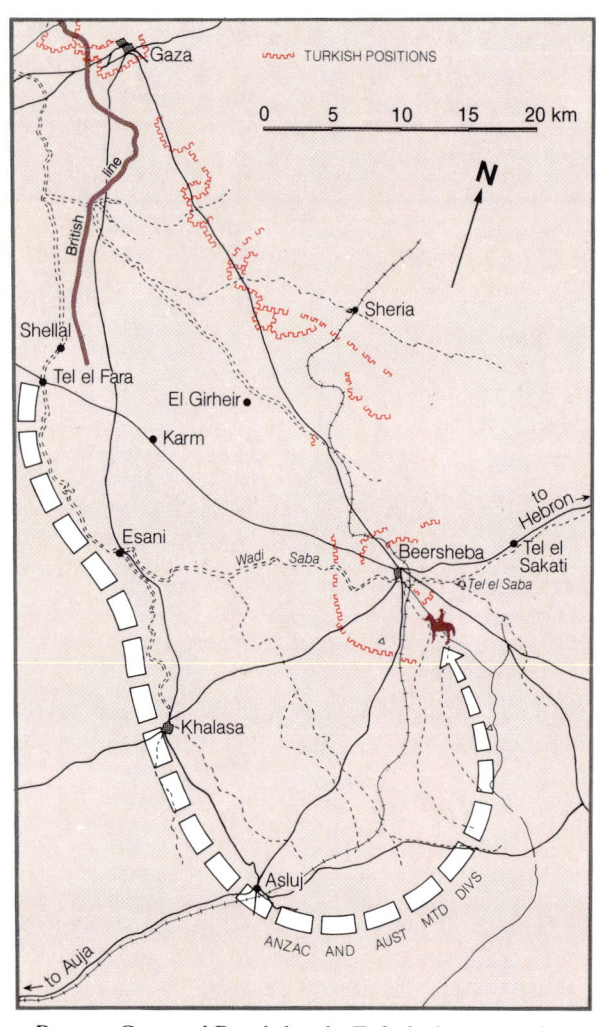

Between Gaza and Beersheba, the Turks had constructed a chain of formidable redoubts in dominating positions. Gaza itself was surrounded by trenches and barbed wire and was practically unassailable. Beersheba, at the other end of this defence line, was strongly fortified to the west but had inferior entrenchments and no barbed wire on its eastern side. Chetwode's plan involved the Light Horse in an encircling movement to capture Beersheba from its vulnerable eastern flank.

ranged these Philistine hills. Most were stone-lined and 6 to 30 metres deep. They were classified on the light-horsemen's maps in terms of the number of camels they could water – 100 camels for some, 1,000 camels for others, and, for a few, 1,500 camels. A couple were marked "plentiful". And the wells of Beersheba were shown as "unlimited". The town lay in the centre of the drainage basin of the Wadi Saba, which flowed down from the Hebron Hills and went on to feed the Wadi Gaza.

The authors of Genesis cannot agree whether the patriarch Abraham or his son Isaac named Beersheba. In the Abraham version, his herdsmen argue with Philistines over the ownership of a well. A treaty is struck, commemorated by naming the well Be'er Sheva, the Well of the Oath. In the Isaac version, the finding of water coincides with a treaty. The details are unimportant. The essential fact is that Beersheba had always been water rich. In October 1917 its 17 wells were held by the Turks, and any army that tried to take Beersheba would have to advance into the drylands and depend on the surrounding 100-camel and 1,000-camel wells. The scattered, limited water-points could support only a small force. So Beersheba was considered safe from any major attack.

Less than 20 years before, Beersheba had been almost a ghost town of the desert fringe. But Turkish and German enterprise had revitalised it as an important railway centre. Handsome public buildings, including a mosque, hall of government, post office and hospital, had been built from the pale local stone around a square segmented with lawns and gardens. An orange grove, plantings of peppercorn and gum trees, large reservoirs and an aerodrome completed its transformation into what propagandists called the City of the Prairie.

Two Turkish lancer regiments and four regiments of infantry were stationed here under Lieutenant-Colonel Ismet Bey, newly arrived from Syria and described by General Liman von Sanders, who had commanded the Turkish forces on Gallipoli, as "one of the most capable of the higher Turkish commanders." In the last week of October, the garrison would be stiffened by a regiment of crack storm troops from the Germanised Yilderim (Turkish for "Thunderbolt" or "Lightning"), the force raised for the recapture of Baghdad.

Two of Ismet's other regiments were made up largely of local Arabs and, in the eyes of the Turkish staff, "could not be considered of much value." But they were mainly farmers and, defending their own fields, they would prove formidable. The Turkish staff also forgot that Arabs revered Abraham as their ancestor, and Beersheba had been founded by Abraham. His original well and the tamarisk tree he planted beside it could be seen near the wadi at the edge of town. The infidel would not win these sacred places cheaply.

After their first failure at Gaza, Murray and Dobell had considered an attack on Beersheba, at the other end of the line, but the water problem had seemed insoluble. Now, Chetwode, Dobell's successor, produced his "Notes on the Palestine Campaign," a brilliant and often witty blueprint for the breaking of the Turkish line. Chetwode's idea was to convince the Turks that there was to be a third attack on Gaza, make a surprise attack on Beersheba, gain water and higher ground, then roll back the line, redoubt by redoubt, and force the Turks from Gaza.

Water for the attack remained the only flaw in Chetwode's scenario. But, on May 22, a massive operation against a Turkish railway line from Beersheba to Asluj in the south helped solve that problem. While the entire Imperial Mounted Division and two brigades of Anzacs engaged the Turks south of Beersheba, parties of engineers would blow up the line and several stone viaducts. The operation went like clockwork. And it also enabled a survey of water sources at Khalasa and Asluj, both major sites of antiquity. Chauvel estimated that, with a fortnight's work, they could supply enough water for two divisions. A mounted advance to Beersheba was possible. The remarkable tactical jig-saw was taking shape.

During the Asluj operation, another piece dropped into place, unnoticed. Forsyth's old regiment, the 4th Light Horse, had at last joined the Desert Column, under a new young commanding officer, Lieutenant-Colonel M.W. ("Swagman Bill") Bourchier. Regarded as a patched-up remnant of the original regiment, the 4th faced a huge body of Turkish cavalry at Asluj; however, the untried Bourchier handled the cunning desert fighters with Chauvel-like calmness and shrewdness. He feinted with a dismounted bayonet charge while sending mounted men in a threatening sweep to one flank. Taken by surprise, the Turks pulled back, surrendering a commanding ridge.

As the light-horsemen were returning from their mission on May 24, a British officer made a dramatic entrance to Cairo. He was a powerful 39-year-old man in the brand-new uniform of a major and he carried a Zulu war club as a swagger stick. He showed some interest in the Savoy Hotel, where General Murray had his headquarters, and in Shepheard's Hotel, where the overflow of officers shuffled papers and sipped drinks under the ceiling fans and palms. He also sought out Jewish refugees from Palestine, rode out into the desert supposedly to study birds and was seen consorting with Bedouin, whom he disliked, and later with Lawrence of Arabia, whom everyone disliked. His name was Richard Meinertzhagen, a mystery man, who, almost inevitably, would be arrested briefly as a spy. In a way, that is precisely what he was: head of Field Intelligence for the new Commander-in-Chief, General Sir Edmund Allenby.

Two weeks after Meinertzhagen's arrival, General Murray was told that he was being replaced. And on June 27, Allenby arrived in Cairo. The poet Banjo Paterson, who was in command of a Light Horse remount unit in Egypt, knew Allenby from the Boer War. Paterson described him as a "well set-up man at least six feet high, and broad and strong as a London policeman." Paterson was obviously delighted as the "the Shepheard's Hotel generals were dispersed with scant ceremony. Army headquarters . . . were moved a hundred and fifty miles or so nearer the enemy. 'We're a bit far from our work up here,' said the big man. 'I'd like to get up closer where I can have a look at the enemy occasionally.'" Five days after his arrival, Allenby left to inspect the battle lines in his staff car, "a great lonely figure of a man," said Paterson, "riding in front of an obviously terrified staff."

Historian Henry Gullett recalled that Allenby "went through the hot, dusty camps in his army like a strong, fresh, reviving wind. He would dash up in his car to a Light Horse regiment, shake hands with a few officers, inspect hurriedly, but with a sure eye to good and bad points, the horses of perhaps a single squadron, and be gone in a few minutes, leaving a great trail of dust behind him." The Light Horse loved him. Like the men in France, they called him "the Bull." The big question was whether Chauvel would retain his command under Allenby. A brigadier scoffed, "Fancy giving command of the biggest mounted force in the world's history to an Australian. Chauvel's sound, but he's such a sticky old frog." But, as Paterson commented, "Allenby didn't care whether a man were an Australian or a Kick-a-poo indian; he wanted to win the war." The Desert Column became the Desert Mounted Corps, incorporating the Anzac Mounted Division, the Australian (no longer Imperial) Mounted Division, the Yeomanry Mounted Division and the Imperial Camel Corps Brigade. And Chauvel was placed in command with the rank of lieutenant-general, the highest rank then achieved by an Australian.

Meanwhile, Allenby enthusiastically took up

THE COMING OF AL-NABI

When General Sir Edmund Allenby made his triumphal entry into Jerusalem in December 1917, it seemed to many Arabs that he was fulfilling an ancient legend – a great prophet would come from the west and enter the city on foot to bring peace and prosperity. The Arabic word for prophet was *al-Nabi*, and that was how Allenby's name was translated by the Arabs. He was hailed as a messiah whose conquest was seen as the will of Allah.

To the troops under his command, he was known as "the Bull," partly because of his hefty physique but also because of his notorious outbursts of rage. Senior officers were known to have been physically sick after interviews with him; one collapsed on the floor in front of his desk and had to be carried from the room. Allenby himself admitted to a friend: "I want to get this war over, and if anything goes wrong I lose my temper."

Yet he was also a sensitive man with an abiding interest in literature, music and natural history, especially ornithology. His biographer, Brian Gardner, wrote that "here was a General who could quote Milton's *Comus* at length and who would break off a discussion about strategy to discuss roses, French literature, the habits of birds, and, incredibly, Crusader castles."

Allenby hated war. A military career was not even his first choice, but having failed as a young man to gain entrance to the Indian Civil Service, he sat for the Royal Military College at Sandhurst and passed. After 10 months he was commissioned in the Inniskilling Dragoons and sent to South Africa. And it was in South Africa, nearly 20 years later, that Allenby, then approaching 40, saw his first action, at the Boer War.

The Boer War transformed Allenby into a dedicated soldier. He had been shocked by the incompetence of his superiors and was determined to put matters right and instil common sense, imagination and thoroughness into military strategy. But incompetence still marked British commanders' conduct of affairs in World War I. Allenby himself came in for criticism over his handling of the Battle of Arras. Nevertheless, it was his forcefulness and reputation as a cavalry commander that led to his appointment as Commander-in-Chief of the forces in Palestine.

After the war, Allenby was appointed British High Commissioner in Egypt, a position he filled with firmness and discretion until 1925. In 1919 he was raised to the peerage, becoming Viscount Allenby of Felixstowe and Megiddo. But to the Arabs he would be remembered as al-Nabi, and to the troops he would remain the Bull.

General Sir Edmund Allenby in Palestine.

Flanked by representatives of the Allied nations, General Allenby stands on the terrace below the Tower of David in Jerusalem while his proclamation of martial law is read.

Chetwode's plan for the strike at Beersheba. He brought in reinforcements, more and better artillery, more and better aircraft, and started to push the railway and pipeline eastwards. But the key to the plan was making the Turks believe that the next strike would be at Gaza, so that Beersheba could be taken quickly in a surprise attack. Artillery sites were prepared near Gaza and an army corps was moved into position with only pretended security, as a dummy railway terminal was built. Warships prowled off shore, and the garrison on Cyprus created a stir, suggesting an amphibious assault from that quarter. The Turks were wary and got ready for another attack on Gaza. But they also sent another division to Beersheba.

Now came Major Meinertzhagen's great moment. He prepared some fake documents which showed that there would be a feint attack on Beersheba to cover the third assault on Gaza. A British officer dropped them in Turkish territory on September 17. But they were not found. A light-horseman dropped a second carefully prepared package on October 1. Again the Turks failed to pick up the bait. So Meinertzhagen made the third attempt himself, determined that this time there would be no mistake.

In a combined wallet and notebook, Meinertzhagen placed an agenda for a conference on the proposed Gaza attack and the accompanying feint against Beersheba by a couple of brigades. He also included a letter from an officer friend criticising the high command for not launching a full-scale attack on Beersheba, and a copy of a signal to the Desert Mounted Corps advising that an officer from general headquarters would be passing through their sector. He put £20 in the wallet to help confirm that this was an accidental loss, and packed it all in a haversack with his lunch, which he also planned to lose. As a final stroke of near-genius, he enlisted the aid of "a little hospital nurse at El Arish with girlish handwriting", as another intelligence officer described her, and coached her to write a remarkably moving letter, supposedly from his wife, describing their recently born son. This was carefully folded and refolded many times to appear much read, then added to the collection in the haversack.

On October 10, with a rifle and water bottle, Meinertzhagen set off on horseback into the Turkish side of no man's land. "After crossing the Wadi Gaza," he recounted, "I turned northwest towards Sheria. I rode handsomely, and not far from El Girheir I found a Turkish patrol which immediately started chasing me. After about a mile they stopped, so I also stopped and fired on them at a range of about 600 yards. That annoyed them and they came on again, firing as they rode, but without doing any damage. This was my chance and I tried to remount, letting go of my haversack, binoculars and water bottle. I also dropped my rifle which I had stained with fresh blood from my horse, doing everything to make them believe I had been hit and was trying to escape for dear life. When they came close enough I abandoned the haversack in which was my notebook, various maps, lunch etc. and rode off. I saw one of them stop and pick up the haversack and rifle and then I was off like the wind."

The Turks were wary of a ruse, and the authenticity of the find was much debated. But a German intelligence officer, Captain Schiller, pointed to the letter about the baby. "It is a letter in a million. Its loss could only be accidental." Von Kress was likewise convinced. The division he had moved into reserve at Beersheba was hastily moved back to Gaza.

On October 15, five days after Meinertzhagen had dropped his decoy material, von Kress visited Beersheba. He mentioned the pocket book and its key documents to Ismet Bey, telling him, "Beersheba can be subjected to an attack of one of two infantry brigades and cavalry from the west and from the south of the Wadi Saba." And he added: "It is impossible that large mounted forces will operate from east of Beersheba." But Ismet remained wary. This talented officer set about improving his defences on all fronts, including the east, and made elaborate preparations for demolition. First, all the wells and water storages were wired with explosives, then demolition charges were set in

Men and their walers assemble on the rocky plain outside Beersheba before the battle.

ammunition dumps, railway carriages and locomotives, the mosque and the town's flour mill. By the last week of October, Beersheba would be primed like a gigantic bomb – a death trap for any invader.

Allenby had set Z-day for October 31. Before this, while a massive bombardment was concentrated on Gaza, Chetwode's infantry would move out in secret night marches and prepare to attack Beersheba from the south and west, while the Desert Mounted Corps circled far down to the south and then moved in on Beersheba from the desert flank – the east. Despite the new water points at Khalasa and Asluj, the attacking horsemen would still face a 43-kilometre ride from water to launch the attack. Beersheba's wells had to be gained in one day. And they had to be captured intact.

On the eve of the Beersheba attack, the Light Horse suffered what could have been a grave blow. Some time before, during a gas exercise by the 3rd Brigade, Galloping Jack Royston had deliberately inhaled some poison gas so he could be sure of recognising its presence. He became seriously ill and, after some time in hospital, was ordered back to England. On October 30, he officially surrendered command to Brigadier-General Lachlan Wilson, former commanding officer of the 5th Light Horse Regiment, already leading his new brigade towards Beersheba. The Light Horse had lost a supreme leader. But only one day later they would perform an exploit to out-Royston Royston – the ultimate 11th-hour attack. A new legend would be born, built around not a single great figure but the common soldiers of the Light Horse, and their walers.

The advance to Beersheba began for most light-horsemen in the late afternoon of October 28. With freshly watered horses carrying three days' fodder, they rode away from the setting sun, full water bottles slung under their arms, three days' bully beef and biscuits in their haversacks. Riding silently, four abreast, regiment followed regiment in a huge column more than 16 kilometres long, snaking out of the hills around the Wadi Gaza, then across the flatlands towards the south-east and the rising full moon. Behind them, the decoy bombardment on Gaza flashed and rumbled like a sheet lightning.

A few men rode overnight to Khalasa, 30 kilometres away, to prepare for the next halt. Most stopped at Esani, after a 16-kilometre journey. A week before, Ryrie had brought his brigade there to help develop the water supply. Now it was a bountiful water point.

Men and horses rested in wadis the following day; then, towards nightfall, they struck forward again, the Australian Mounted Division halting at Khalasa while the Anzacs pressed on to Asluj, another 16 kilometres on. Here, Ryrie had found that "all the wells had been blown up and were full to the top with rocks and rubbish." Working parties of 250 men took 24 hours simply to clear the debris. Now, despite a further week's work by engineers, encouraged by a visit from Allenby, the water supply was still below expectations.

Some horses would drink at Asluj, many would not, as the advance continued in its last and most critical night march of 40 kilometres (56 kilometres for the Australian Mounted), swinging up into the tangle of hills and wadis east of Beersheba. Despite the problems with water, by 5:10 a.m. the advance guard of the Australians had linked with the Anzacs as they moved into a loose crescent of positions among the hills, Anzacs poised for their attack, Australian Mounted in reserve. The hills crumpled down to a broad valley plain about five kilometres long, beyond which, on slightly rising ground, a sprawl of mud huts surrounded a group of larger buildings and the white minaret of the mosque, gleaming against a background of bare, brown hills scribbled with trenches. At 5:55 a.m. the British artillery

LIVING AND FIGHTING ON HORSEBACK

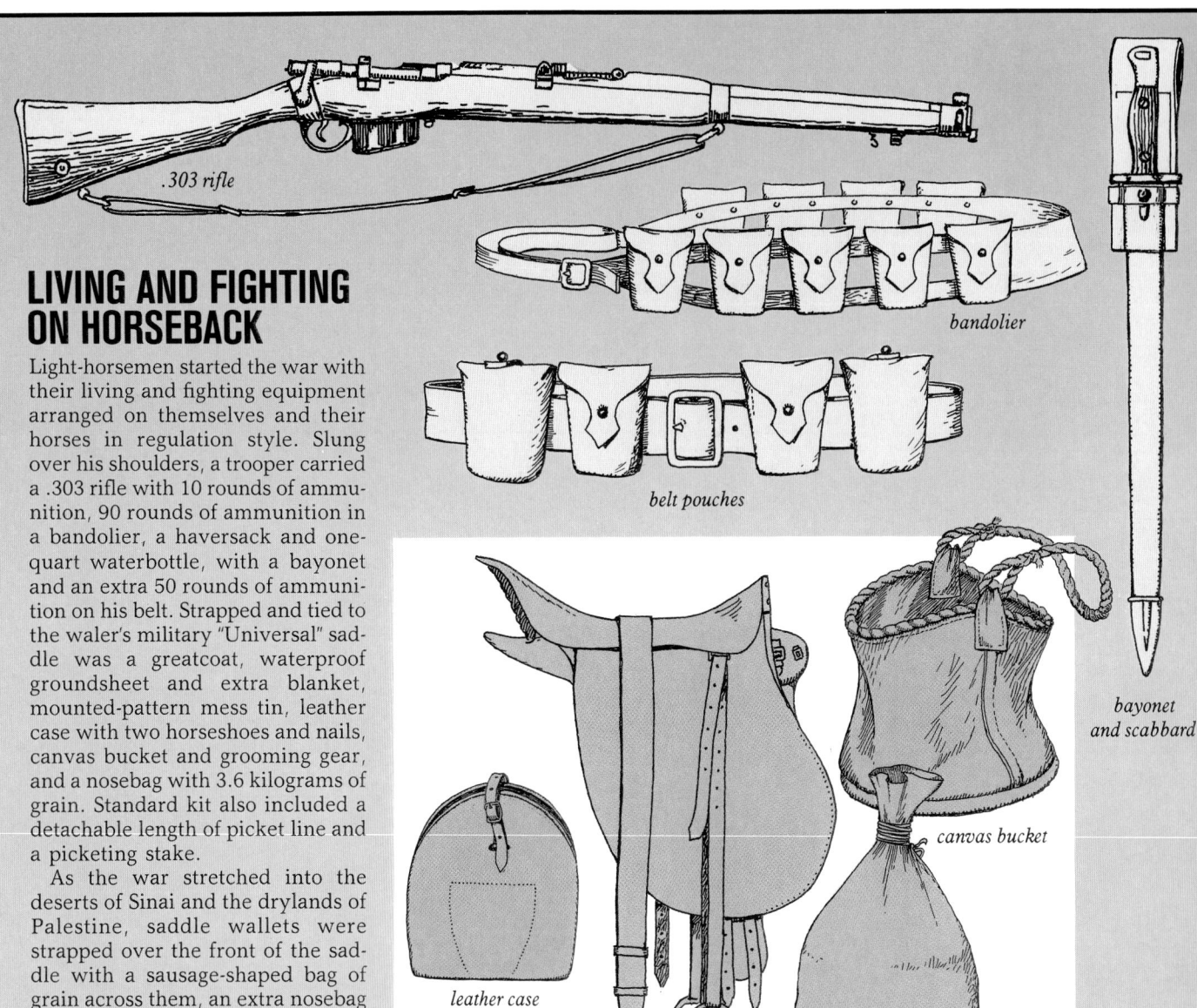

Light-horsemen started the war with their living and fighting equipment arranged on themselves and their horses in regulation style. Slung over his shoulders, a trooper carried a .303 rifle with 10 rounds of ammunition, 90 rounds of ammunition in a bandolier, a haversack and one-quart waterbottle, with a bayonet and an extra 50 rounds of ammunition on his belt. Strapped and tied to the waler's military "Universal" saddle was a greatcoat, waterproof groundsheet and extra blanket, mounted-pattern mess tin, leather case with two horseshoes and nails, canvas bucket and grooming gear, and a nosebag with 3.6 kilograms of grain. Standard kit also included a detachable length of picket line and a picketing stake.

As the war stretched into the deserts of Sinai and the drylands of Palestine, saddle wallets were strapped over the front of the saddle with a sausage-shaped bag of grain across them, an extra nosebag and water bottle were slung from the saddle, a spare bandolier hung across the horse's neck, and a leather muzzle was fitted to stop it from eating sand. The tethering headrope was often replaced by a chain, and long sticks called "bivvy poles" were carried to aid in the erection of makeshift shelters.

Each man rigged "full marching order" to suit himself, and saddles became so heavy with gear that only the stronger men could lift their loaded saddles without help. Late in 1918, a trooper described himself loading his horse "till the mount looks like a very creditable imitation of a Christmas tree." Another commented that some saddles were so crowded with gear "you could hardly see where a man could fit." It was not by the book, it did not look neat, but it worked. To the Light Horse, that was all that mattered.

rolled greatcoat wrapped in groundsheet

blanket

water bottle

canvas haversack

launched their bombardment. The battle of Beersheba had begun.

The light-horsemen smoked their morning pipes and gave their horses a nosebag; the Anzacs checked their equipment for mounted action. Many of the horses had already been 20 hours without water; some had not drunk for 36 hours. And there was a day of battle ahead, in building heat.

While Chetwode's infantry advanced on the Turkish trenches to the west of Beersheba on a 4.5-kilometre front, the Light Horse prepared to attack the eastern defences, a rough crescent of trenches and redoubts with two formidable strong points — fortified hills called Tel el Saba and Tel el Sakati — which commanded all approaches. The New Zealanders would attack Tel el Saba while Ryrie and the 2nd Brigade moved on Tel el Sakati and the main road to Jerusalem via Hebron.

"The country is quite open," Ryrie wrote, "and there is no cover and overlooked by high hills; so the only way was to go at it." He went on to describe the attack: "We raced across the open and soon the Turks started a barrage of shells across our front but we never stopped. We raced through the Bedouin camps scattering sheep, goats, turkeys, fowls, the women wailing and kids howling and shells bursting everywhere made me laugh. We saw three old Bedouin knocked over but it was extraordinary how few men and horses of ours were hit. I think our sudden dash at them made the gunners shoot very wild. The Turkish prisoners all say they are terrified of the Australian cavalry."

The 7th Light Horse Regiment under Lieutenant-Colonel George Macarthur Onslow was leading the brigade in its widely scattered dash across the flat when a regiment of Turkish lancers with four field guns galloped out into the open, then wheeled for Tel el Sakati. Onslow and his men spurred to cut them off, but the Turks reached the fortifications and swung their guns into action. This extra fire from rising ground forced Onslow and the following regiments to cover in a wadi, and they began a grim, slow, dismounted advance. Ryrie had been galloping in pursuit of Onslow to direct him in the attack. Now he wheeled and rode back to bring up artillery support, later confessing, "I'm afraid I was rather rude to some young artillery officers for not being quick enough. However, they did good work when they got started and knocked out three of the enemy guns."

The brigade commanded the Hebron road and captured 10 bullock wagons of fodder before eventually taking Tel el Sakati at 1 p.m. Meanwhile, to the south, the New Zealanders were tackling the more formidable Tel el Saba, a miniature plateau bristling with entrenched riflemen and machine-guns. They faced the same wild gallop under artillery fire, the same dogged advance, while British gunners tried to knock out the machine-guns. As the advance edged on, Chauvel sent the 1st Light Horse Brigade in support.

In Beersheba, Ismet Bey was waging his own battle with von Kress. A Turkish staff officer would comment, "Von Kress had only one solution for the enemy's attack and opposed all others. His whole conduct was based on the contents of the pocket book which had lately come into his hands." From early morning, Ismet had known that this was no mere feint by a couple of brigades, and he estimated the strength of the attack with considerable accuracy. Towards noon, aerial reconnaissance confirmed that "besides infantry there were two to three cavalry divisions in the east, one to one and half in the south." He informed von Kress by phone, but the gaunt Bavarian was adamant. "No. There are only two cavalry brigades."

Holding in his anger, Ismet then gave a detailed report of the situation and asked von Kress for orders. They came back: "Beersheba will be held. The battle will continue." There was no mention of reinforcements, of counterattacks or of evacuation. So, with only 4,400 men and 28 field guns, Ismet Bey continued to hold off the attack by 58,500 men and 242 guns. To the west and south, British infantry had occupied his major line of defence; to the northeast, the bastions of Tel el Saba and Tel el Sakati

For this Turkish patrol, captured outside Beersheba before its surrender, the fighting is over.

were being overwhelmed. He sent his few available reserves to the eastern trenches facing the open valley plain and the hills beyond, where most of the enemy cavalry were dispersed. His planes made repeated bombing attacks and kept the horsemen scattered under cover in wadis. Ismet's only ally was time.

Chauvel, stationed with his staff on a high ridge, below the corps pennant, was increasingly uneasy. The remarkable panorama of battle lay before him, its details pinpointed by frequent phone messages. The passing of time was uncomfortably marked by the swing of the sun from behind his left shoulder, to overhead, and then in steady decline towards Beersheba.

At 3 p.m. Tel el Saba fell after a superb bayonet charge by the New Zealanders. The 1st Brigade, on the left, now began their move on the Turkish trenches. Another slow, dismounted advance. Allenby's orders were clear: to take Beersheba by nightfall. Chetwode, originator of the Beersheba plan, had gained most of his objectives, and there was always the uncomfortable possibility that he might forestall the Light Horse in the final strike at the town.

There was another pressure on Chauvel. Banjo Paterson explained that an Australian general "who had married into the English aristocracy and thought himself next in order for the cavalry command" had come along to Beersheba with his orderly. The general told Paterson, "This chap Chauvel . . . he's too damn slow. I've just come along to see how things turn out." But the most pressing problem, of course, was water. Many of the horses had not drunk for nearly 32 hours; some were already nearly 48 hours without water. Unless the Desert Mounted Corps could take the wells of Beersheba intact by the time night fell at 5:30 p.m., the horses faced a killing 12-hour march back to Khalasa or beyond.

Chauvel called General Hodgson and his officers of the reserve Australian Mounted Division to conference on his hilltop. When he put the situation to them, Brigadier-General William Grant of the 4th Brigade, a tall, handsome, impulsive officer, said that he believed his men could take the town, asking, "Will you give me a free hand, sir?" Chauvel weighed the question momentarily. "Yes, but as I am responsible for your actions, I must know what you intend." "A cavalry attack, sir," Grant coolly replied. At this, Brigadier-General P.D. Fitzgerald of the Yeomanry stepped forward, suggesting that if there was to be a cavalry attack, it should be made by his men, who were armed with swords. Again, Chauvel hesitated fractionally. Then he turned to Hodgson and said quietly, "Put Grant straight at it." It was now about 4 p.m. The sun would set at 4:50 p.m.

Almost precisely as Grant and his officers were leaving Chauvel, six kilometres away, in Beersheba, Ismet Bey saw that further resistance was futile. He ordered "a general retirement towards the north of the town," covered by an eastern rearguard. But at the same time he sent the 27th Divisional Engineer Company "to destroy the water supply." He was defeated but would deny victory to Chauvel.

Everything now depended on the speed with which Grant could make his plans, gather his men, and launch his charge. These mounted infantrymen would be attempting something unheard of in modern warfare – a cavalry charge across nearly five kilometres of open ground against an entrenched enemy supported by artillery, machine-guns and aircraft. Even if it could be mounted in time, even if it could be executed by men unequipped and untrained for such action, riding horses that had been without water for 32 to 48 hours, how could it succeed without appalling losses?

Grant designed his attack with characteristic decision. His two closest regiments, the 4th and the 12th, would make the charge. The first two of each regiment's three squadrons would be in "squadron line extended" – riding abreast; the third would be in "line of troop column" – eight parallel lines, each of one troop. Lieutenant-Colonel Bourchier of the 4th Light Horse would lead both regiments. Lieutenant-Colonel Donald Cameron of the 12th would ride with his C Squadron and attached Vickers machine-gunners to protect the charge formation from Turkish positions on high ground to their left. The 11th Regiment, which was farthest away, would move up as soon as it was possible and follow as a reserve.

While squadron leaders rode off to muster their regiments from the wadis where they were dispersed, Grant, his brigade major and the two commanding officers, Bourchier and Cameron, selected a forming-up area – a broad hollow straddling a road, screened from Beersheba by a ridge. They then scouted an approach route along a wadi bed which would protect the gathering regiments from artillery fire.

Back in the wadis where the 4th and 12th Regiments were scattered, it had been a dull and frustrating day, the horses waiting saddled, heads bowed in the heat and dryness, the men listening to the sounds of battle, noting the passing of afternoon. They were not heroes; as far as most of them were concerned, they had been lucky not to see action. But their bottles were empty or nearly empty. And the horses needed water. Suddenly, the squadron leaders were cantering back among them. "All pack horses to the rear. Remainder prepare for action, see that all equipment is securely tied to your saddles." Then the order "Mount!", and they swung into their saddles, formed up four abreast, and cantered off along the wadis, by troop, squadron and regiment. Most men did not know what was happening. Some guessed. Trooper Fowler of the 12th heard his troop leader call, "We expect to water our horses in Beersheba tonight!"

By about 4:30 p.m., 20 minutes before sunset, the 4th Regiment was cantering out on to the deployment area to form up its three squadrons in the charge formation. As soon as they were deployed – horses four or five metres apart, and about 300 metres between each of the three squadrons – Bourchier led them off at the walk-march, moving to a slow trot. Already, luck was with Grant. Bourchier, most of his officers, and the nucleus of his first and third squadrons were

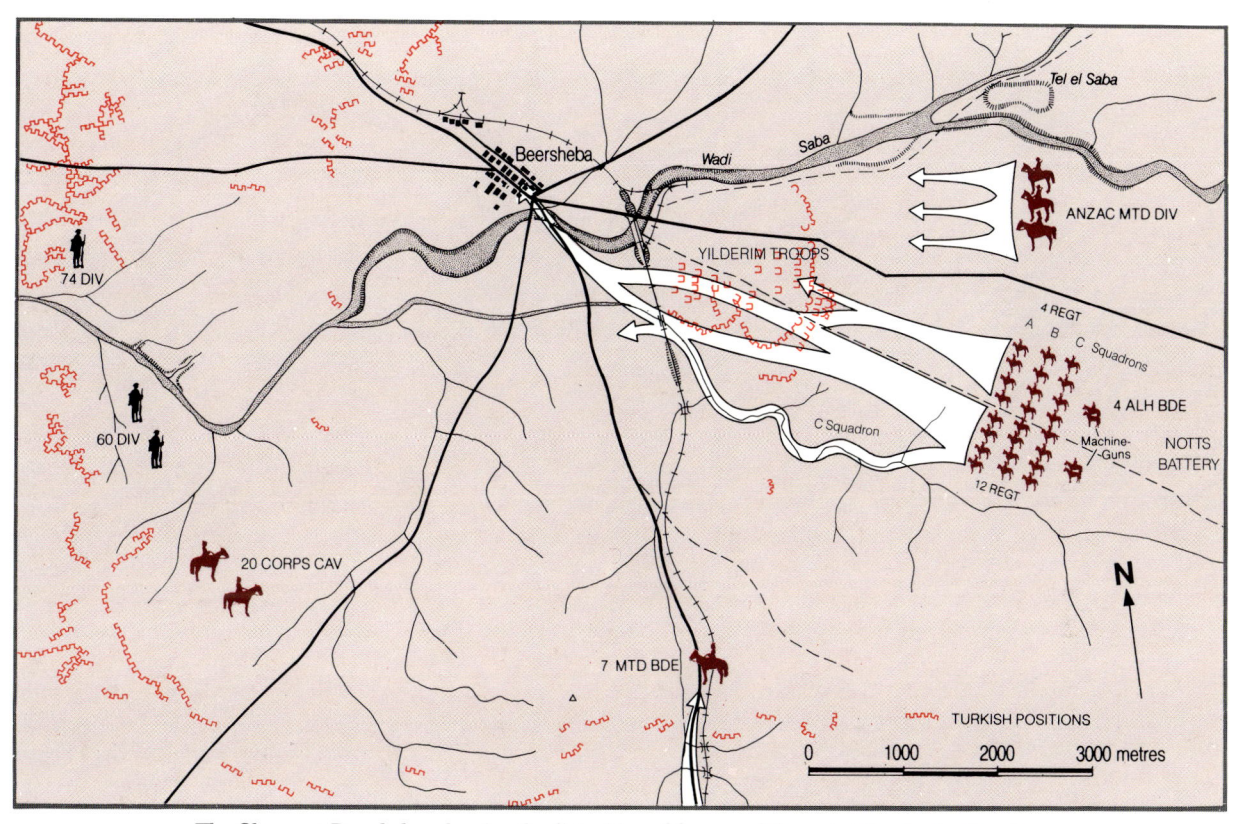

The Charge at Beersheba, showing the disposition of forces and the route taken by the charging squadrons of the 4th and 12th Regiments of the 4th Light Horse Brigade.

4th Light Horse "originals" who had trained in Dad Forsyth's mad Egyptian charges nearly three years before. They established formation, direction and pace in true cavalry style. Meanwhile, the 12th Regiment had reached the start line and was forming up. It then set off, caught up with Bourchier's men, and aligned its three squadrons with those of the 4th to their right.

The charge formation of some 800 horsemen crossed the screening ridge, squadron by squadron, and trotted down to the rubbled valley plain, a regiment to each side of the road leading towards the minaret of Beersheba's mosque, six kilometres away. They had to ride about three kilometres to the first Turkish trenches.

Almost as soon as they moved into the open, a Turkish outpost opened fire from a hill to their left rear. Finding himself under heavy rifle and machine-gun fire at a range of less 800 metres, Cameron of the 12th swung his C Squadron and the machine-gunners to cover in a wadi and dismounted to attack the enemy position. But by now, the Notts Battery had arrived at the charge's start line, and Grant quickly directed its fire on the Turks. Although firing straight into the setting sun, the British gunners silenced the enemy with their second shot.

It was now too late for Cameron and his men to rejoin the charge. He led his small force along the wadi and attacked another Turkish hill post that had opened fire on the left flank of the formation. Down on the flat, astride the Beersheba road, Bourchier had increased pace to a canter, and the men of the two regiments held their horses in hard as the animals smelt water ahead and strained into the dying sunlight.

From the Turkish trenches, the lines of cantering horsemen, stretching 1,100 metres across the broad, gently sloping valley, were a daunting sight. But they were recognised as light-horsemen – mounted infantry – and the order was given, "Wait until they dismount, then open fire!" Then suddenly, just under two and a half kilometres from the trenches, Bourchier signalled the charge. The horses lunged to a gallop and the three lines were hurtling across

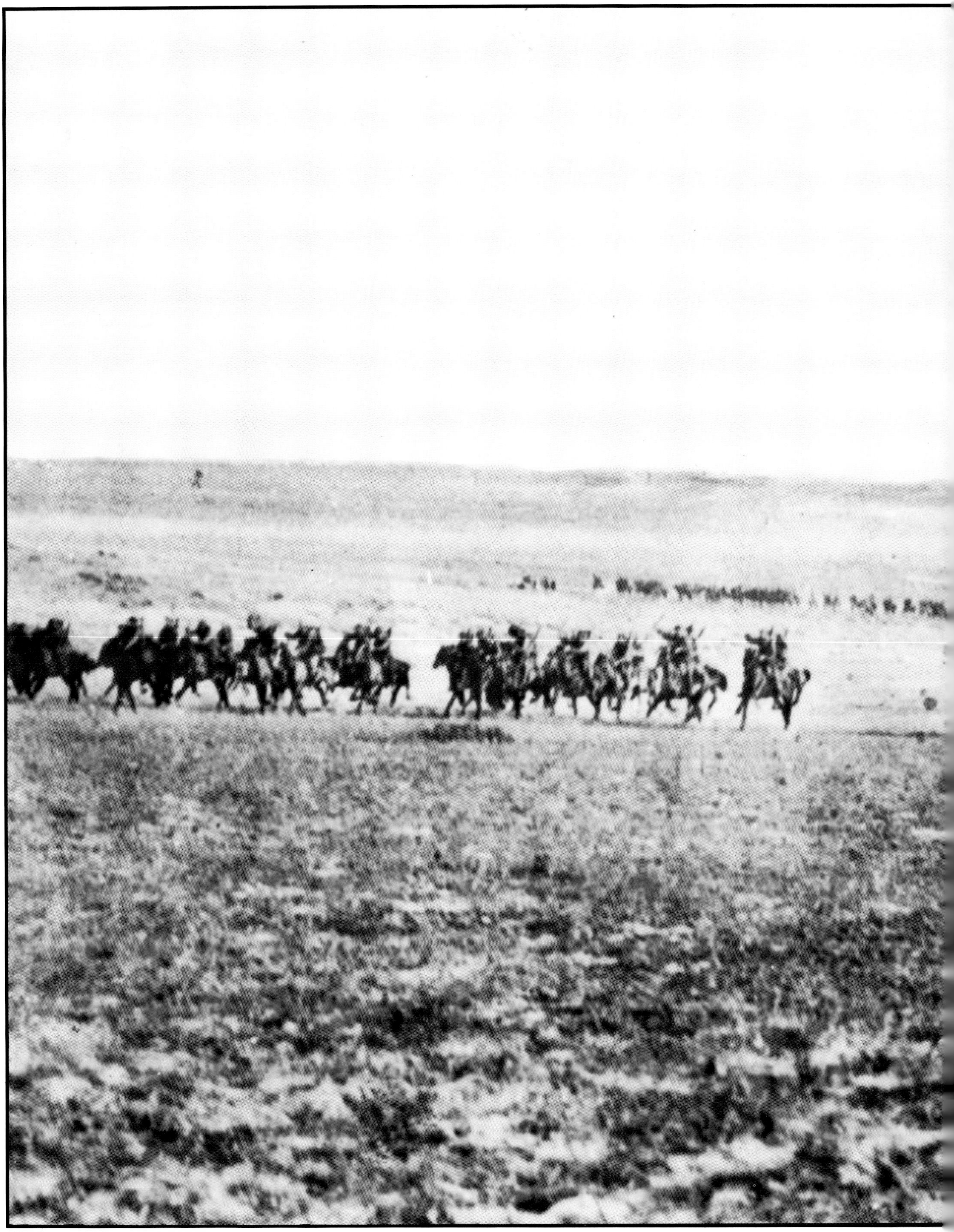

Men of the 4th Light Horse Brigade begin their great charge at Beersheba on October 31, 1917. This historic photograph was taken by an advance scout, Eric Elliott, who stopped and trained his camera on his companions.

the rock-strewn rubble, the men yelling wildly – stock yells, coo-ees, even laughter – and drawing their bayonets to flash their sharpened blades in the coppery sunlight.

Immediately, three batteries of Turkish artillery opened fire with high explosive and shrapnel. They had followed the range of the advancing formation, winding their guns down, waiting for the halt and dismount. The first shells exploded among the galloping lines, scattering shrapnel from air bursts, pluming dust and smoke from ground bursts. Horses and men fell, but the charge swept on at impossible speed, the light-horsemen lying flat on their horses' necks. One trooper remembered being irritated because his horse kept its head low, offering no cover. Another recalled glancing aside to see that his mate had an eye hanging out on one cheek, and watched helplessly as he clung to his saddle for a hundred metres, then fell to the ground. Then, after a brief zone of casualties, the lines were galloping free, with shells falling behind them. The Turkish gunners could not wind their trunnion wheels fast enough. The charge was under the guns.

Two German planes that had been rearming swooped to meet the horsemen with bursts of machine-gun fire and dropped bombs that exploded harmlessly between the plummeting squadrons. At about a kilometre and a half from the trenches, a dozen machine-guns and a thousand rifles opened fire. Again, men and horses were hit. Some horses fell; others kept galloping, though mortally wounded, bursting their hearts to keep pace with those to either side. Trooper Bert Hutchinson of the 4th Regiment watched the tiny, winking flame of a machine-gun brightening as it came directly into line with him. Then his troop leader, Lieutenant Frank Burton, blocked the ugly little sparking and crashed to the hard ground as his horse stumbled. Galloping behind Burton, Trooper Lindsay Taylor saw the lieutenant lying dead as he flashed past, then he turned ahead, flat on his horse's neck, watching its ears flicking as machine-gun bullets whistled around them.

Riding with the 12th, Trooper Fowler recalled, "The machine gun and rifle fire became intense. As we came in closer to the trenches, some of the Turks must have forgotten to change the sights on their rifles as the bullets went overhead." Every man who rode in the charge had the same experience. Even the Turk, one of the world's great defensive fighters, was rattled by the incredible spectacle of the galloping squadrons, the flashing bayonets. Every rifle picked up after the action would have its sights still set on 1,500 metres.

But, as the first line thundered closer to almost point-blank range, bullets were again cutting down men and horses, Trooper Phil Moon of the 4th Regiment said, "We can feel the concussion of the fire in our faces.... I got my head down on old Jerry's neck and was doing some mighty deep thinking. Next to me, Johnson's horse gets it through the head and Johnson takes a tumble."

Nine men of the 12th, whose horses were shot immediately in front of a formidable redoubt, took cover in broken ground and opened fire. The remaining 20 men of their troop veered to the left and tried to gallop through a narrow gap in the defences. Only six horses made it, the last of them ridden by Fowler. "About 20 yards to my left, I could just see as a blur through the dust some horses and men of the 12th Regiment passing through a narrow opening in the trenches. I turned my horse and raced along the trench. I had a bird's eye view of the Turks below me throwing hand grenades etc. but in a flash we were through with nothing between us and Beersheba."

Another troop of the 12th, with two Hotchkiss machine-guns, dismounted in front of the redoubt to engage the Turks. Survivors of the remaining six troops galloped across the shallower trenches to the left and charged through 500 metres of scattered rifle pits and dugouts before reining in on the banks of the broad Wadi Saba to consolidate for the ride into Beersheba. The pause would allow Ismet Bey to escape.

To the right, the leading squadron of the 4th, commanded by Major James Lawson, had hit a succession of trenches and dugouts manned

*Horses leap the trenches of the dismayed Turks in George Lambert's graphic portrayal of
The Charge of the Light Horse at Beersheba.*

by the formidable Yilderim storm troops. Two scouts galloping 50 metres ahead had gone straight through them, miraculously unharmed. Bourchier and Lawson led A Squadron at the first bow-shaped trench as a salvo of stick grenades tumbled through the air, wiping out three of the four men in one section. From one troop, only six or seven men crossed the first trench on horseback and 14 of the 28 horses were killed. The squadron galloped through a jumble of bell tents and dugouts, then jumped the second trench, two and a half metres deep and well over a metre wide. Some Turks stabbed up at the horses with their bayonets; many surrendered, but snatched up their rifles again as the light-horsemen dragged their horses to a halt and most dismounted.

In a shambles of mounted men wheeling back with bayonets in their hands, horse holders leading mounts clear, and men running back to the trench with fixed bayonets, a hand-to-hand fight began – the most vicious between Australians and Turks since the landing at Gallipoli. In at least four separate incidents, light-horsemen were killed by Turks who had already surrendered. Trooper Moon was with his troop leader, Lieutenant Ben Meredith, as he dismounted. "He hands his reins over to me and turns with his revolver on one of these pits full of Turks. They throw up their hands at once, but as he turns away one of them picks up his rifle and shoots him in the back." Moon did not say what happened next. Other light-horsemen told how he bayoneted the Turk, again and again, yelling "You bastard! You bastard!" The other Turks who violated their surrender also died.

Bourchier fought among his men at the trenches, killing six Turks with his revolver in that brief, ugly battle. Lawson led his squadron at a redoubt nearly three metres deep, running through rifle and machine-gun fire to engage 100 Turks. All the Turks were killed or captured, and Lawson would be recommended for the Victoria Cross.

Amazing images leapt from the dusty chaos: a man pinned to the ground by his dead horse, swapping shots with a Turk, killing him; a trooper grazed by a bullet, swung off-balance by the weight of ammunition and haversack, spinning, as his mate laughed; the corpse of Regimental Sergeant-Major Alec Wilson still riding his big charger; a waler joining the fight, rearing to lash out with its fore-hooves.

A few troopers of the 4th Regiment had galloped straight through the Turkish defence and joined men of the 12th as they rode into Beersheba amid "a terrific sustained roar" of demolition explosions – ammunition dumps, a flour mill, a locomotive blown end over end, and the first two of the precious wells. The German officer in charge of the demolition was on leave in Jerusalem, but another engineer had the vital job. Unfamiliar with the system and with some wires broken by artillery fire, he was detonating the charges at random, operating a switchboard in the town's central square.

That officer – "dark-haired, good-looking and clean – about 25 or 26," an Australian recalled – probably never knew that for the next few moments the fate of Allenby's campaign and the entire future of the Middle East were in his hands. A few twists of wire and flicks of a switch could destroy the desperately needed water supplies and turn the British victory into a debacle. But two light-horsemen, Troopers Hudson and Bolton of the 4th, rode over and bailed him up with "a blood-curdling yell." Startled, he leapt to his feet and surrendered, with only two of the crucial wells destroyed, two damaged, and reservoirs holding 400,000 litres of water still intact.

As darkness fell, 58,500 men and 100,000 animals swarmed in on Beersheba. It took 1,800,000 litres of water to slake their battle thirst. One man remembered watering his horse at a Turkish canvas trough and falling on his knees in the water to drink beside it.

History's last great cavalry charge had saved an army and set it on the way to Jerusalem, with only 31 men killed and 36 wounded. At least 70 horses had died. About 40 were scattered along the course of the charge; others had carried their riders to the trenches before they collapsed; some had fallen at the wadi near small pools of water.

In the years ahead, the men of Beersheba would talk briefly of that magnificent and terrible action and tell of the death of mates with dry eyes and a regretful cock of the head. But for the horses that died that day, there would be a moistening of the eye and a silence of memory. As one light-horseman would say, "It was the horses that did it; those marvellous bloody horses. Where would we have been but for them?"

SHOT IN COLOUR

A pilot and observer of No. 1 Squadron, Australian Flying Corps, compare notes in front of a Bristol Fighter aircraft in Palestine. Australian airmen successfully prevented German reconnaissance planes from observing Allenby's preparations for the Great Ride.

With one trooper scanning the enemy line and another using a range-finder, a team of 3rd Regiment light-horsemen take up their positions with a deadly Vickers machine-gun.

A PHOTOGRAPHIC ADVENTURER

For more than 50 years, the glass plates of the only colour photographs taken of British Empire forces on active service in World War I lay undisturbed in the protective darkness of the Australian War Memorial in Canberra. They were the work of one of the world's great adventurer photographers, Frank Hurley.

Hurley had been the photographer with Douglas Mawson's Antarctic expedition in 1911-13. A year later he was back in Antarctica with Sir Ernest Shackleton's ill-fated expedition, enduring incredible hardships and recording the exploit on still and moving film.

It was not until he and the other members of the Shackleton expedition were rescued in August 1916 that Hurley knew World War I had started. By mid-1917, however, he had been appointed an official war photographer and was recording the rigours of war on the Western Front and later in Palestine with the Light Horse and the Australian Flying Corps.

Colour photography was in its infancy at the time and available to relatively few experimenters in the field. Hurley, in the vanguard of experimental photography, used the French Paget process, invented about 1908, which made use of a system of screens within the camera, each absorbing a certain colour.

After the war, Hurley continued his adventurous photographic career, accompanying Ross and Keith Smith on the Australian leg of their historic flight from England and making further photographic expeditions to Antarctica as well as to other remote places of the world. In World War II he was again commissioned as an official war photographer and served with the Australian Imperial Force recording the war in the Middle East.

Hurley's photographs of the two world wars form an important part of the War Memorial's collection of more than half a million pictures. His colour work, which was rediscovered during a stocktake in the late 1970s, is notable for its clarity, which is all the more remarkable considering the stage of development of colour photography at the time of World War I.

Light-horsemen take it easy in their desert camp at Ashdod in January 1918. Following the capture of Jerusalem, nearly all the Light Horse were sent for a spell to Ashdod and Belah, near the Mediterranean coast. "Although a season of winds of almost hurricane force made life in the canvas bivouacs somewhat sporting and uncertain," wrote historian Henry Gullett, "the men, now expert at makeshifts, were on the whole snug, well-fed and happy."

*A camel ambulance stops to pick up a wounded man at Rafa.
The swaying cacolets astride the camels' humps provided uncomfortable transport for the injured.*

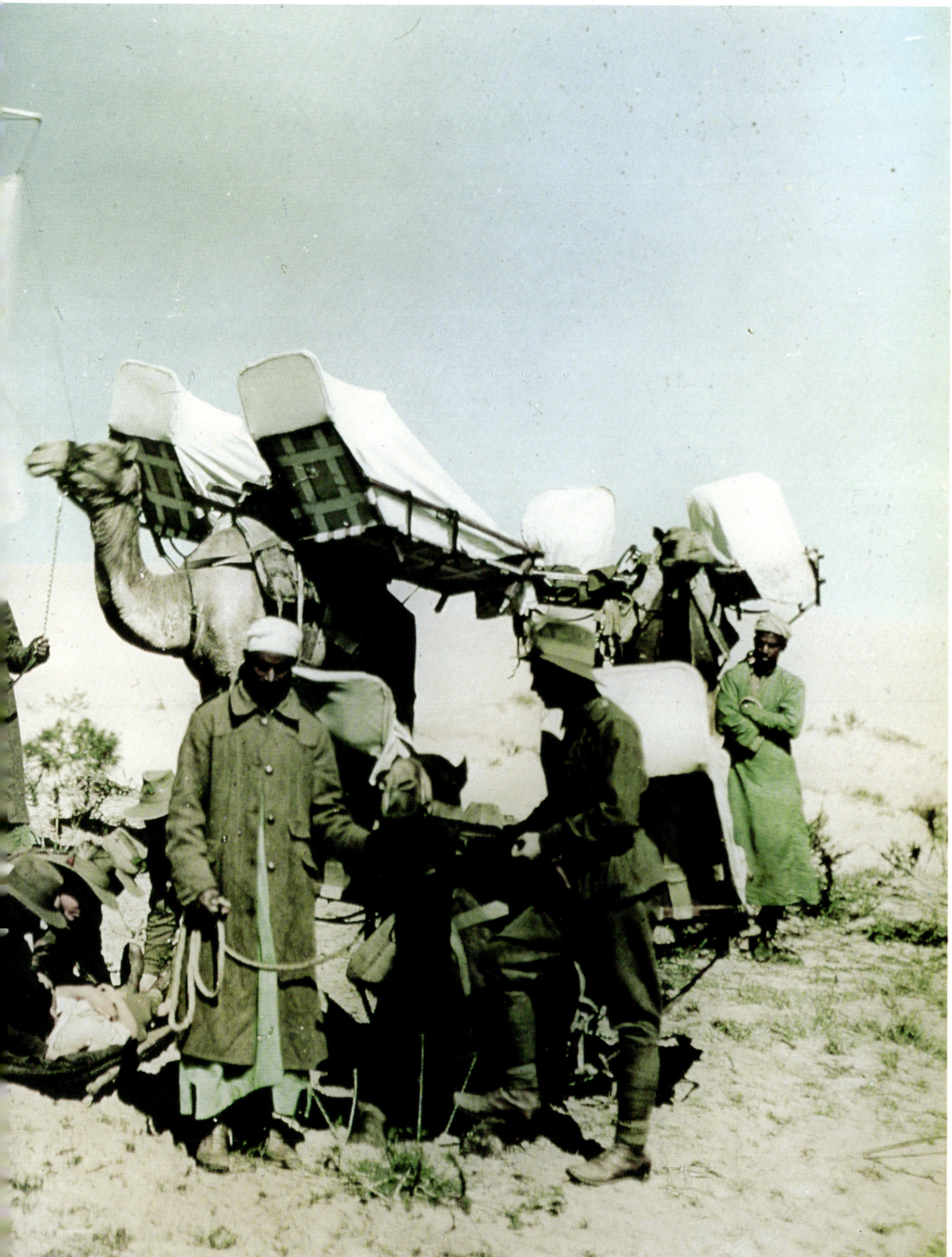

Snipers of the 3rd Light Horse Regiment man a lookout post at Khurbet Hadrah, part of the front which swept in an arc from Jerusalem to the coast north of Jaffa.

A convoy of field guns and their tractors and limbers makes a roadside camp on the Jericho road ascending from the Jordan Valley.

Light-horsemen stroll round part of the Old City of Jerusalem during the lull in operations before the advance into the Jordan Valley. Frank Hurley subsequently produced a popular book of photographs of Jerusalem.

A veteran light-horseman gathers anemones growing wild at Belah. The winter rains which had swollen the Jordan gave rise to a brief blooming of spring flowers in the desert.

Gathering a different kind of ground covering, photographer Frank Hurley examines shells left by the Turks in their hurried retreat from Katia in August 1916. Although the Light Horse attack on Katia had to be called off, the Turks were forced to abandon the town.

4

DEADLOCK IN THE EAST

With Beersheba captured, Gaza soon fell. The Light Horse now began to push the Turks back into the rocky Judaean Hills, and after a gruelling winter campaign, Jerusalem was taken. Then came the furnace-hot pest hole of the Jordan Valley.

The fall of Beersheba launched a dizzing phase of the campaign. Allenby's tactics were designed to keep the Turks guessing as he hit and feinted from right and left along a 48-kilometre line, threatening to strike at Gaza and towards Jerusalem from Beersheba while his main assault would roll back the Beersheba-Gaza line. But, almost immediately, unforeseen problems threw him off balance, making his moves even more unpredictable.

Water, as ever, was the key problem. Allenby's huge force of infantry, Desert Mounted Corps and artillery — 58,500 men — was draining the supposedly unlimited supply at Beersheba. A hundred motor lorries, each with a 1,800-litre tank, shuttled to and fro, day and night, between Beersheba and the head of the pipeline at Karm, 26 kilometres away. Then a hot wind started to blow, drying the few pools in the wadis, increasing the thirst of men and horses. In choking dust, thousands of horses jostled around the wells of Beersheba. One day, cameleers waited nine hours, then drove their mounts among the horses to frighten them away and snatch a drink. Another 800 camels arrived in the town after

From the sketchbook of George Lambert.

six days without water. Stories drifted in of infantrymen fighting in the hills, water bottles empty for 36 hours.

The massive feint attack on Gaza had now developed into an all-out assault, ripe for the planned strike north-west from Beersheba to knock out the Turkish line, redoubt by redoubt. But Chauvel's horsemen, with their enormous watering problems, were not ready. And while von Kress battled to hold Gaza, the Turkish Seventh Army under Fevzi Pasha prepared to recapture Beersheba.

Von Kress expected the Light Horse to strike north-east from Beersheba towards Jerusalem. A brilliant feint by a unit of 100 Arab auxiliaries under a British officer seemed to confirm this line of advance, and six battalions were hurled against the minuscule unit, weakening the defence of Gaza. But the ruse backfired. Chauvel now needed the wells at Khuweilfeh, north-east of Beersheba, and part of this massive force blocked him, beginning an ugly battle in which, uncharacteristically, the Turks deliberately shot stretcher-bearers and camels carrying wounded. "Khuweilfeh was a horrid show," said Trooper Humphrey Kempe of the 3rd Light Horse Regiment, recalling "the sort of fear that is hard to throttle" as he and his mates battled all day among naked, stony ridges, then raced back to Beersheba for water. "Supplies were limited and our mounts had somehow to be dragged away before satisfying an appalling thirst, while others which could smell the splashed water would, lunging with screaming neighs, put up a real performance. Troughs being of canvas . . . had to be treated with care and, while horses jostled, thrashed about and reared, others would charge into the scrum. There seemed to be a writhing mass of heads, limbs, bodies and tails, more like a writhing mass of snakes than quadrupeds."

Chauvel had to send the entire Australian Mounted Division back 26 kilometres to water at Karm. As a consequence, a planned attack on the Turkish redoubts north-west of Beersheba at Hareira and Sheria was postponed from November 3 to November 6. When the attack was finally launched, British infantry advanced across the same wretched bare slopes faced by the light-horsemen seven months before. The Turks were already withdrawing from Gaza, which fell on the morning of November 7, and as soon as the centre of the line was broken, the plan was for the Light Horse to push through and cut off the enemy retreat near Huj.

The light-horsemen watched the British infantry attack on November 6 from reserve positions behind the artillery. Then, early next morning, the British captured the main Turkish position at Sheria and the Light Horse rode forward. The Anzac Mounted Division struck north-west through the broken Turkish line and began to overtake retreating Turks. Wrote Trooper Kempe: "It was highly exciting galloping through the enemy who gazed in consternation and made little attempt to stem our victorious and quite ecstatic advance."

Further south, at Wadi Sheria, more determined Turks had blocked the gallant Londoners of the 60th Division, and the Australian Mounted Division was sent to clear the way. Chauvel ordered a direct frontal assault on the Turkish position and gave the attack to Grant's 4th Brigade. After an unexplained delay of nearly three hours, the 11th and 12th Regiments formed up for a Beersheba-like charge and started off at the trot, moving to the gallop as they came under fire. A trooper recalled, "We could see hundreds of dead and dying Londoners of the 60th Division, with stretcher bearers attending them. Our horses had some trouble in passing them, as they lay so close together on the ground."

Lieutenant-Colonel Cameron, commanding officer of the 12th Regiment who had led a squadron to cover during the Beersheba charge, again halted and dismounted one of his two squadrons in a wadi, leaving the other to continue for a few hundred metres before it too reined in. Turkish fire now concentrated on the squadrons of the 11th Regiment, and

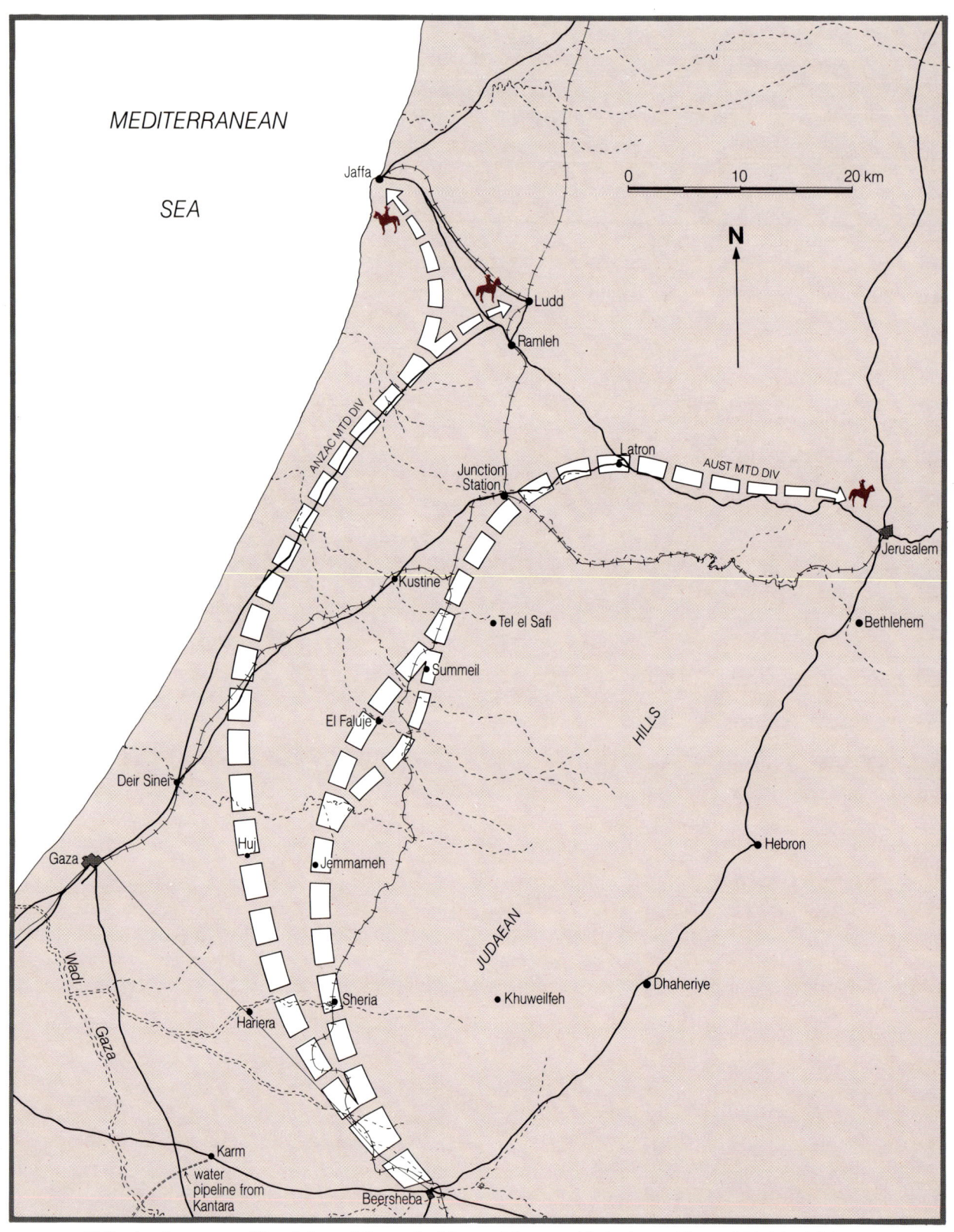

Following the capture of Beersheba and Gaza, the drive north began, with the Anzac Mounted Division joining the British infantry in the advance up the maritime plain, and the Australian Mounted Division sweeping north and east towards Jerusalem.

Squadrons of the 4th Light Horse Brigade halt among the ruins of Gaza. Not only was Gaza damaged by British shellfire; the Turks themselves systematically wrecked houses to obtain timber for their trenches.

they also halted, except for a single troop led by 23-year-old Lieutenant A.R. Brierty, who carried this remnant of the charge home. Some Turks surrendered as the 21 horses leapt their trench, but the tiny, unsupported group was hopelessly outnumbered and surrounded. The horses were shot down as Brierty and his men made a pathetic stand, helped only by a few mates from the 11th Regiment who advanced with a Hotchkiss gun. Later, the regimental padre, Chaplain W.J. Dunbar, made a heroic attempt to rescue one of Brierty's men, but they were both killed by machine-gun fire.

That evening, the reserve brigade of the 60th Division advanced through the dismounted squadrons of the 11th and 12th Light Horse Regiments and took the Turkish position with a bayonet charge. But the delay had been fatal to Allenby's hope of smashing the Turkish army as it retreated from Gaza.

Chauvel has been criticised for ordering the attack as he did. And it is true that two Light Horse regiments could have suffered the fate of Brierty's troop. But it is equally possible that they could have shaken the Turks into surrender and opened the way for a stunning early victory.

The following day, November 8, the Desert Mounted Corps continued its attempt to cut off the Turkish retreat in the face of dogged rearguard action. That afternoon, the Londoners of the 60th Division were confronted by eight field guns and three howitzers escorted by infantry and machine-gun crews. Lieutenant-Colonel H.A. Cheape of the Warwickshire Yeomanry, a master of foxhounds, led a splendid charge by 10 troops. Though mauled by shrapnel and machine-gun fire, the Yeomanry spurred at the guns with hearty British cheers. The Austrian gunners fired until the last moment and set their shell fuses at zero to make them burst at the mouth of the guns and act as grapeshot. The British official correspondent reported that every gunner was cut down at his gun "in true Balaclava style." The action threw into high relief the previous day's failure at Sheria by the 11th and 12th Light Horse. But, of 170 Yeomanry who had made the charge, 75 were killed or wounded and 100 horses were lost.

That same day, the 3rd and 10th Light Horse attacked the Turkish flank guard in position along the Wadi Jemmameh. Major A.C. Olden of the 10th Regiment reported: "The high ground on the north side of the wadi held a series of redoubts which were held in force by the Turks, whilst the wadi bed – almost a mile wide – appeared to be alive with snipers." After a steady advance, driving the Turks from one redoubt after another, the 3rd Regiment and two squadrons of the 10th charged the final positions, scattered the Turks and took several guns, with a handful of casualties. But it was too late. Most of the Turks had escaped Allenby's net.

Mass movement of the Light Horse was now increasingly hampered by lack of water as they found many major water points destroyed by the retreating Turks. Scouts and intelligence patrols were constantly hunting for wells and cisterns. Sometimes whole regiments were watered at crude wells where buckets had to be hauled up with ropes, the operation taking eight hours or longer. Now it was commonplace for horses to be 48 and even 60 hours without a drink. Regiments detoured 15 kilometres to find water, and clashes with Turkish rearguards became almost incidental. The adjutant of the 4th Regiment reported a typical water search by four troopers under Sergeant Syd Vialls: "They first visited Uzzie, a small railway station which possesses a well with engine attached for lifting water, but as the essential parts had been removed was of no use. When close to the station, an enemy sentry attempted to shoot them but Vialls shot him and with Trooper Atkins rushed the house where they captured 10 of the enemy; these were sent back to the Regiment under escort of Trooper Johnston. The sergeant and the other three then pushed on for about two and a half miles towards Tel el Safi until they ran into an enemy screen, two of whom they captured, then they continued in another direction until water was discovered."

Despite the battle for water, despite the delays in the start from Beersheba, despite the superb Turkish rearguards, by November 10 the Anzacs had linked with British infantry advancing up the coast, and the Desert Mounted Corps formed a great scythe blade across western Palestine, from the Judaean Hills to the sea.

At Junction Station on the main north-south railway, a branch line ran east to Jerusalem. It marked a point of decision for both armies. The Turkish Eighth Army continued its fighting retreat up the coast, faced by the Anzac Mounted Division, while the Seventh Army, which had failed in its attempt to retake Beersheba, drew back into the Judaean Hills towards Jerusalem, opposing the Australian Mounted Division. On the maritime plain the Anzacs found fertile country and scattered Jewish villages, with orange groves and vineyards. Many a trooper continued the advance with a spare water bottle filled with wine. Allenby's main thrust was on this coastal flank. But the Turks were still wary of the hill road from Beersheba to Jerusalem, and the Australian Mounted's advance into the Judaean Hills was hard fought. Now Allenby chose his moment, launched a massive feint up the coast with his left, then, as the Turks counter-attacked, struck with his right towards Jerusalem.

The Judaean Hills were rocky and steep, their slopes terraced by Arab farmers with rock retaining walls. This gave valuable cover for a man fighting uphill but created a cruel obstacle course for horses. An officer reported, "Several times during the day the troops were forced to ascend or descend well over 1,000 feet. Occasionally it was necessary to climb on all fours and the plucky horses would follow like well-trained dogs."

PRIDE – AND PREJUDICE

By the time the war had dragged into its third and fourth years, the light-horseman had developed a very clear view of himself – and others. It was a view devoid of false modesty – or of much modesty of any sort, for that matter. He had become a "Billjim," mirrored in his own magazine, *Kia Ora Coo-ee*, as "tall, brown, broad-shouldered, deep-chested, clean-shaven, with a lazy, slouching gait like that of a sleepy tiger, and calculating eyes. Easygoing mostly, he is full of surprises when roused."

He admired the fighting ability of the London infantrymen, but his praise often sounded patronising, mingled as it was with comments on their small stature and poor sense of direction. But there was nothing patronising in his view of the Scots. He found the Scot honest, intelligent, radical, frank and intolerant of military pomp but, above all, what one trooper called "the most fierce and pitiless fighter in arms."

The light-horseman was loud in his contempt of the Arab as an ally never to be trusted, and was bitterly frustrated by standing orders that forbade retaliation against Bedouin helping the enemy. Yet many of the Turkish soldiers he respected were Arabs – reluctant conscripts herded off to war like cattle. A Turkish uniform transformed the detested Arab into a respected enemy.

In the same way, the light-horseman's loathing of Egyptians never extended to men of the Egyptian Transport Corps and Labour Corps who worked and died beside him. He praised their courage and was moved by the Egyptians in the freezing Judaean Hills who curled up beside their dead camels and simply let go of life. The uniform robe with its embroidered "E.T.C." was a shroud to many Egyptians carefully buried by light-horsemen. They were a funny lot, the Billjims.

Top: Scottish infantrymen, popular with the Light Horse, march in easygoing fashion across the sand. Above: A group of Bedouin and their mounted guard smile for the camera, though relations between Arab and light-horseman were rarely amicable.

As they climbed higher, men who had been riding in shirtsleeves pulled on their tunics. Then the autumn rains set in, day after day of steady downpour that quickly soaked through woollen greatcoats and turned every track into a creek, every gully into a torrent. Transport wallowed to a halt in gluepot bogs, and many men were left in the hills with whatever food they were carrying. It was impossible to dig trenches in the rocky ground, and defensive positions were set up behind "sangars", loose rock walls about a metre high, which provided some shelter from wind-driven rain as well as bullets. A Judaean Hills "bivvy" was a sitting-stone set against the sangar, with a ground sheet thrown over the top of the wall then draped down over head and shoulders. Most men had no blankets and had to sleep under saturated greatcoats. At least they kept the wind off. But then it grew colder.

Trooper Fowler of the 12th Light Horse Regiment recalled: "Around 9 p.m. my feet would start to throb and about 11 p.m. the pain was almost unbearable, and towards 2 a.m. there would be no feeling at all in the feet, and they were hard and cold as stone and the pain next morning in getting some feeling back was just agony." Fowler and the 12th Light Horse had marched into the Judaean Hills to relieve the Scots Fusiliers near El Burj for one night. They stayed for nearly five weeks, losing men with frostbite, manning the sangars by night, leaving a skeleton force by day while they tried to sleep.

As supply problems increased, all horses were sent back, except those of the 10th Light Horse; on November 20 the regiment had received word that they would represent Australia in the final assault on Jerusalem – as mounted troops. They rode towards the sound of battle passing many dead British infantrymen, burying those they could at each halt. Then, on November 21, during a patrol by A Squadron, the sheikh of the village of Soba took squadron-leader Major C.G. Dunckley and some of his men to a hilltop and pointed

General Allenby makes his entrance into Jerusalem on December 11, 1917, flanked by troops from all countries involved in the campaign. A proclamation was immediately read guaranteeing protection for all sacred places.

to the east with a joyous cry of "Shouf! El Kuds!" ("Look! Jersualem!"). "There, over line after line of terraced hills covered with olive trees and vines, with the limestone road winding its way in and out of them like a tiny white thread, could be seen the glistening domes and spires of The City of Our Dreams."

Ahead, the 75th Division of English and Indian troops had lost two-thirds of its men. Now the remarkable Londoners of the 60th Division came marching up from the plain, still in their summerweight uniforms and shorts, bare knees bandaged against the cold. The 10th Light Horse Regiment were attached to the Londoners and protected their right flank, eventually to link with the British 53rd Division coming up the road from Beersheba. The regiment would then advance between the two British infantry divisions in the final strike at Jerusalem, set for 5:15 a.m. on December 8. Allenby had issued strict orders that "no advance should be made against any resisting enemy within the boundaries not only of the Holy City but of its suburbs." Jerusalem must be unscarred by battle.

After magnificent work by the Egyptian Labour Corps, roads had been upgraded for heavy traffic. But the broad-padded camels which had negotiated soft mud could not retain their footing on hard, slippery surfaces. So 2,000 donkeys became the link between lorry limits and the front line, unperturbed by shellfire, happy to feed on anything that grew.

Despite a fierce storm on the night of December 7, the 10th Light Horse, together with the Worcestershire Yeomanry, were able to fill the gap between the two British divisions, ready for the final assault on Jerusalem the next morning. The Light Horse advance was spearheaded by a six-man patrol under Lieutenant Tom Rickaby, whose shirt had been stained by the rusty lance head a few months before. They came under heavy Turkish machine-gun fire and galloped through rain and mist up a slippery slope to take cover behind a stone wall and send their horses to shelter in a quarry. The six light-horsemen held their position all day, exchanging shots, until the Turks withdrew in late afternoon. That night, British infantry moved into the Turkish position.

Early next morning, December 9, word flashed through the British lines that Jerusalem had surrendered. The Turkish army had withdrawn from the city, supposedly to save its sacred places from battle. That evening, at about 7 p.m., the 10th Light Horse Regiment rode up the winding roads and cavalcaded into the Holy City through a drizzling dusk, with heavy artillery firing over their heads at the Turks to the east. They were the first mounted troops to enter the city.

In this strange moment of triumph, soured by wet and cold, the people of Jerusalem offered a welcome described by Major Olden of the 10th Regiment as "something of a half-timid, half-wistful nature." They were uncertain of the future, short of food, and most lacked even oil or tallow to burn in their lamps. All the more remarkable was the image recorded by Trooper Henry Bostock: "We passed a house where the occupants were holding a dance in what appeared to be a large verandah with glass sides and well lit. They were all dressed in full evening dress, both men and women. Truly a sight to remember on such a memorable night."

The regiment took over the Turkish cavalry barracks, and their walers, after weeks in mud and rain, spent the night dozing in cosy stalls. Some men slept in mangers. Perhaps, so close to Bethlehem and Christmas, their resting place meant something more than dryness and rough comfort. One commented simply, "It was the most appropriate thing to do."

On December 11, after a day of skirmishing and patrols, the 10th Regiment supplied part of the guard of honour at the Jaffa Gate for Allenby's official entry. At high noon he rode up with his staff, then dismounted and entered on foot, without flags, trumpets or drums, walking through the gateway called by the Arabs "the Friend." Christian, Jew and Moslem cheered him.

Meanwhile, fighting as infantry from the stone sangars of the Judaean Hills, the Light Horse had helped beat back a major Turkish attempt to cut off the Jerusalem strike force. As Christmas approached, the weather and the supply problem grew worse. One freezing night, Red Hutchinson of the 4th Regiment was crouched with his mates behind their sangars. "There was just a small party of us and there was a bit of an attack on our flank — not immediately on our front but close to us. And we thought we were next. About midnight, we heard the skirl of bagpipes. It was Scotties from the 52nd Division coming up to take over. They hopped in and ended the Turkish attack. I like the bagpipes but they've never sounded the way they did in the hills that night. It was the most beautiful sound I'd ever heard. It was salvation."

That was a Christmas long-remembered by the light-horsemen. Colonel Bourchier, temporarily in command of the 4th Light Horse Brigade in "the bleak, cold, wet hills of Judaea", would write: "My only covering was two bivvy sheets, with the rain pouring in through the holes and our clothes wet through, blankets and all, day after day. And to top all this, all we were living on was bully

With Brigadier-General Cox at the head of the column, the 1st Light Horse Brigade file down the Judaean slopes on their way to Jericho.

beef and biscuits. It rained so hard on Christmas Day that we went without our dinner, such as it was, and all had a strong toddy of rum and went to bed in our clothes."

Allenby beat back a determined Turkish counter-attack on the Holy City and by December 30 held a line that ran north of Jerusalem and curved up to the coast north of Jaffa. It was a stunning achievement, representing two months of almost superhuman effort by mounted troops and infantry. He now insisted on time for his men to regain their fighting wind while the worst of winter passed.

Many of the Light Horse were given a spell near the coast at Belah, south of Gaza. To the walers, underfed, tired and sore-legged, it represented their first chance in weeks for "a decent roll." An officer recalled: "They rolled and rolled, and kept on rolling until it seemed they would never cease, and on that first night at Belah, after their evening feed, the stable piquets reported, "Every horse is down to it."

At Belah, during a general smartening up, light-horsemen were given formal training in the use of the bayonet as a short sword and a General Staff officer instructed them in a bizarre ceremonial drill in which the bayonet was substituted for the British cavalry sword. The men found this amusing but were less tolerant of an order to restage the charge at Beersheba for the cine camera of the official photographer, Captain Frank Hurley. They resented the idea of reliving that traumatic action and refused to ride full tilt. Even judicious under-cranking by the wily Hurley could not make the mock charge travel at a normal gallop, let alone the headlong pace achieved at Beersheba. It was noted that Bourchier was absent for the re-enactment.

In February 1918, while the Australian Mounted were acting out their charades at Belah, the Anzac Mounted were supporting the Londoners of the 60th Division in the capture of Jericho. The New Zealanders and the 1st Light Horse Brigade set out from Bethlehem and struck down towards the Dead Sea through the tangle of naked brown hills on the eastern slopes of the Judaean watershed. They plodded down goat tracks, alternately riding and leading their horses, while to their left the infantry fought down the main hill road.

The New Zealanders made a dismounted attack on Turkish hill positions which were abandoned after British infantry closed in from the rear. Meanwhile, Brigadier-General C.F. Cox's 1st Brigade had reached the floor of the Jordan Valley near the Dead Sea, 400 metres below sea level, and struck north towards Jericho. A single troop of the 3rd Regiment entered Jericho and found that all but a handful of the garrison had fled. Whatever the light-horsemen had expected of the Biblical city, they captured a squalid little village of mud huts, relieved by a mosque and, as Gullett put it, "the wretched Jordan Hotel, which in days of peace had housed tourists

Troopers of the 3rd Light Horse Regiment gallop into Jericho. The capture of this key town allowed the establishment of a British line along the Jordan.

unfortunate enough to travel without their own camping equipment."

The Anzac Mounted Division had lost only three men. Again, the brunt of the fighting had fallen on the infantry, and, as Gullett noted, "many little crosses bearing the names of Londoners afterwards marked the road from Jerusalem to Jericho." The Turks had retreated across the stone Ghoraniye Bridge before blowing it up. The rain-swollen Jordan now became a 30-metre no man's land between the two armies with Turkish machine-guns hidden among the maze of clay hills and dense undergrowth on the far bank.

Across the Jordan, Allenby already had his eye on the Turkish-held Moab plateau towering more than 1,200 metres above the valley floor – the apron of the vast desert stage on which Arabs loyal to the pro-British Sherif of Mecca were harrying the vital Hejaz Railway to Damascus. By attacking these highlands and destroying a key railway tunnel and viaduct at Amman, Allenby could support the Arab Revolt, isolate the southern Turkish forces, and centre Turkish attention on this eastern flank. He was again preparing to play his left-hand, right-hand, feint and knockout strategy. But first he had to cross the Jordan.

The rain-swollen river was flowing at about 11 kilometres an hour and defeated one night attempt to cross at Ghoraniye. But further south, at the traditional site of Christ's baptism by John the Baptist, a party of naked Australians and Englishmen swam to the opposite bank and hauled a raftload of infantry across under fire. In a night of feverish work and stiff fighting, a pontoon bridge was built by Light Horse engineers, and a company of infantry established itself on the eastern bank. Next day, New Zealand Mounted Riflemen crossed, struck out from the infantry cordon and drove the Turks back to the foothills of Moab, about eight kilometres away. By nightfall, four bridges crossed the Jordan and Allenby could make his strike at the Moab plateau, with the promised support of Lawrence of Arabia and his Arab army to cut off Turkish reinforcements from the south.

Led by Ryrie's 2nd Brigade and the New Zealanders in a two-pronged spearhead, the Anzac Mounted, the Londoners of the 60th Division and the Camel Brigade pushed across to the foothills and started the 1,200-metre climb to Amman and the key town of Es Salt further to the north. An officer wrote: "Immediately we started on the march, the rain commenced. The road was nothing more than a goat track. All night we stumbled along, horses and camels sliding and slipping up and down hills and over stones; it rained incessantly. At 4 a.m. we halted at the head to allow the rear to catch up a little. Being wet through – clothes and blankets absolutely soaked – we lay in the mud until daylight."

The climbing advance continued in steady rain and falling temperatures, men often leading their horses, much of the way in single file. Wheeled transport and artillery were soon abandoned, and the Camel Brigade literally

Troops cross the first pontoon bridge built over the Jordan, at Halja, about six kilometres north of the Dead Sea. By the evening on March 23, four bridges had been built at the two crossings of Halja and Ghoraniye.

dragged their mounts up the treacherous slopes. "The camels were carried up by the men," said General Smith.

After two nights without sleep, the light-horsemen rode out on to the tableland which was now a huge swamp feeding hundreds of small waterfalls. They waited most of the day for the Camel Brigade to catch up, then pushed on overnight and linked with the New Zealanders about 10 kilometres from the main target of Amman. The sun came out and, after three days and nights without sleep, men and horses rested.

That night the railway was blown up to the south of Amman, and next morning the Anzac Mounted and the Camel Brigade made a dismounted attack on the last ridges masking the town. But 4,000 Turks and Asia Korps Germans, well dug in on high ground, met their advance with strong artillery and machine-gun fire. The heavily loaded Londoners now joined the fight after a hellish climb. A trooper recalled: "We saw them come out through the mud, their packs sodden from the rain, their big boots carrying pounds of the sticky soil of the land of Moab. We watched them go, wave after wave, now enshrouded in the smoke of the barrage, now emerging again, the thin lines still thinner, but the slow pace no slower and the direction unchanged."

Meanwhile, the 3rd Light Horse Regiment and British infantry had occupied Es Salt to the north-west and held on despite the threat of Turkish reinforcements marching on them. At Amman, as the battle raged on, great hopes were still held for the advance of Lawrence and his Arabs from the south. "During the Wednesday, we looked in vain through our binoculars," said Captain Rex Hall of the Camel Brigade. "Instead of the Arabs coming, the resourceful German engineers had overnight shaped wooden pieces into the gaps which had been blown by our engineers in each rail, thereby allowing trains with reinforcements to come into Amman."

The first trainload arrived at 3:30 p.m. on Wednesday, and for another three days the appalling battle dragged on. Three troops of the 6th Light Horse Regiment made a bayonet charge and were cut down by machine-gun crossfire. Only one man came back. Trainloads of reinforcements now arrived from the north. A few Arabs appeared, swearing loyalty and cadging food and ammunition. They took their bully beef and bullets and vanished. It rained every day and every night. Each morning, the puddles were crisp with ice.

On the afternoon of March 30, six days after the action had begun, the inevitable retirement was ordered. The wounded left first, most carried on lurching camel-borne litters, some tied to horses, face down on the rump with feet supported by nosebags slung at the shoulders. The whole force had limped back to the Jordan Valley by the afternoon of April 2, nine days after setting out. They had achieved nothing. The Anzacs and the Camel Brigade had lost 671 officers and men; the British infantry, 447. With typical understatement, a trooper commented: "We returned dissatisfied with the operation and depressed at having to leave behind some of our dead."

The light-horsemen had come out of it all with even greater respect for the Cockney infantrymen, even greater contempt for their Arab "allies" and some serious doubts about the legendary Lawrence of Arabia. Captain Hall of the Camels reported: "A week later, GHQ informed us that Lawrence had apologised and that he would be sure to co-operate if Allenby gave him another chance." Incredibly, Allenby did give Lawrence and the Arabs another chance. Within the month, he would strike again at Moab, even though the Turks had more than doubled their forces on the plateau. This time, more than half the Desert Mounted Corps would escape disaster by a horrifyingly narrow margin.

While Allenby's men had prepared to bridge the Jordan on March 21, France had seen a huge German spring offensive and a drive for the Channel ports. The War Office urgently needed 60,000 men from the Pales-

The left flank outpost of the 5th Light Horse wait on the alert at the Ghoraniye bridgehead in the eastern side of the River Jordan. The bridgehead was held throughout the fiery Jordan Valley summer.

tine front to help beat back this awesome assault. Reluctantly, Allenby surrendered two complete infantry divisions and 22 battalions, including most of his Londoners, as well as nearly all the Yeomanry. Later, he would be asked to send another complete division and half of the Light Horse, but at this point he refused. Now he had to rebuild his army — almost entirely with Indian infantry and cavalry — before he could launch his long-planned offensive on the coastal flank. More than ever, it was vital that the Turks should expect his main strike to fall in the east, to give him every advantage of surprise in his coastal offensive. So this became his motivation for the second attack on the highlands of Moab. And he must strike before the rich harvest of the plateau could be brought in by the Turks.

Again, as in the days after Beersheba, a detail of Allenby's tactics seemed at odds with his major aim. On April 18 he launched a feint against a Turkish strongpoint at Shunet Nimrin in the foothills of Moab. This was designed to concentrate Turkish attention on the plateau and draw more reinforcements. Yet only two days later he ordered Chauvel to capture Shunet Nimrin and the key town of Es Salt 16 kilometres to the north-east. This meant that Chauvel would be attacking 8,500 Turks with a force only slightly larger than the one that had failed against 4,000 Turks at Amman and Es Salt. But then, of course, that did not count Lawrence and the Arabs.

Chauvel planned to strike at Shunet Nimrin with the remaining Londoners supported by the Anzac Mounted, while the Australian Mounted pushed 24 kilometres up the east bank of the Jordan, then swung into the ranges to capture Es Salt and cut off the Turks at Shunet Nimrin. To lead it off, the Australian Mounted Division rode up from the coast, through the outskirts of Jerusalem, taking three hours to pass two abreast along the ancient, narrow street. Then they headed down into the Jordan Valley for a brief rest before the advance. The countryside had already dried out after the earlier rains.

On the night of April 29, the huge mounted force clattered across the pontoon bridge over the Jordan, then rode out through the British perimeter. The Londoners were waiting, drawn up in fours, to march on Shunet Nimrin. "As our horses walked swiftly past in the darkness," a light-horsemen recalled, "we

Files of the Anzac Mounted Division extend into the distance as they ride through the outskirts of Jerusalem on their way from the coast to the Jordan Valley. On April 30 they joined the advance on Es Salt.

smothered and half-choked them with the fine white clay dust of the Valley. There were no exchanges of greeting. We rode by in silence. But we were thinking hard, and we thought that, although our gallop up the plain under the Turkish guns at dawn would be no joy ride, we were lucky not to be those little Cockney infantrymen."

Before dawn, Grant's 4th Brigade, as vanguard, struck north through thick scrub. A trooper recalled: "We soon heard, miles away on our right, a splutter of rifle fire, and then a wild outburst of bombing and shafts of the sound of machine-guns. The Londoners had again gone home with bomb and bayonet."

The 4th Brigade moved to a trot on open ground; then, as dawn streamed across the peaks of Moab, Turkish artillery opened fire. The brigade spurred to a gallop and scattered across the rocky plain, followed by the 3rd Brigade. The two brigades engulfed the broken Turkish front line like a tidal wave while artillery fired at random, confused by the thousands of hurtling targets. Trooper Henry Bostock was riding with 4th Brigade headquarters. "Well do I remember galloping past a Turk battery of big guns, with the gun crew standing with their hands up, and some just standing. There seemed to be no one guarding them as we swept past. They would have been taken care of by other units following." In the wild six-kilometre gallop, only six men were killed and 17 wounded. Grant's horse was killed, but he was uninjured and remounted to continue the advance.

The brigade crossed the main road to Es Salt, which ran from Turkish-held Nablus across the nearby Damieh Bridge on their left. Grant found the bridge strongly held by the enemy and spread his men in a flimsy 13-kilometre cordon to check any Turkish reinforcements that might cross the bridge and to protect the vital Es Salt road.

About 7 a.m., Brigadier-General Lachlan Wilson and the 3rd Brigade began the 1,200-metre climb up that road, leaving Grant and his men to guard their escape route. The ride was uneventful until a party of four scouts came to a point where the track split around a large, overhanging rock. Two men crept to each side and killed a Turkish lookout just as he was about to fire at one of the scouts. A second Turk was also killed before he could shoot, but a third man escaped on horseback. Soon afterwards, a cavalry troop scattered ahead of the Australians and the vanguard rode out on to the tableland, knowing that the Turks were ready for them. About a kilometre and a half from Es Salt, the scouts came under fire from a 300-metre redoubt which barred the approach to the town.

After a brief rest for men and horses that had climbed 1,200 metres in 16 kilometres, the 10th Regiment prepared to attack the Turkish position. A dismounted bayonet charge was launched from a ridge opposite the redoubt, two lines of men charging down the near slope and across a gully, while a third line gave covering fire before following. Some of the defenders broke and ran; others met the charge briefly. Then while the mop-up fight was in progress, Wilson waved his red brigade pennant on its lance and the 8th Light Horse started forward at the trot. They quickly spread out, engulfing small Turkish posts, and a troop dashingly led by Lieutenant Charles Foulkes-Taylor, with drawn sword, galloped straight into town down the slippery, narrow, stone-paved streets.

After a brief and scattered fight, the Turks surrendered. Jemel Pasha and his Fourth Army headquarters staff escaped barely a minute before the English forced their way in. A German officer said that the light-horsemen "had galloped their horses where no one else would have ridden at all," and the fall of the town was announced by the remarkable wireless message by the Turks: "Es Salt has been captured by the reckless and dashing gallantry of the Australian cavalry."

It was not yet dusk on May 1 and the operation seemed a stunning success. But to the south-west, at Shunet Nimrin, the Londoners were meeting bitter resistance, and 1,200 metres below the victorious 3rd Brigade, Grant and his 4th Brigade prepared to spend an uneasy night; they knew from reconnaissance that Turkish forces were converging on the Damieh Bridge, preparing to cross the Jordan and attack the mere 1,000 riflemen in their shallow positions scraped from the rocks.

The expected attack came early next morning. But nothing could have prepared the light-horsemen for what happened. Soon after 7 a.m., there was an explosion of machine-gun and rifle fire from the clay hills flanking the Jordan and a huge line of Turkish infantry moved out into the open on a 7,000-metre front. They advanced with parade-ground precision, about 10 metres apart, in unusual dark grey or blue uniforms and wearing German-style steel helmets. A second line followed, then a third and a fourth. Grant's attached British artillery opened fire and blew gaps in the lines. But men from a following line moved up to fill each gap, with almost eerie discipline. By now another five lines had emerged – nine waves of Yilderim storm troops – about 6,000 men in all. Turkish horse artillery batteries galloped out into the open, the waves of infantry started to run, and enemy cavalry speared out on the light-horsemen's right flank.

Grant's right was being driven back, and enemy troops were pouring across a second bridge to his left rear. He had to fall back to a line protecting the vital Es Salt road, until his men were forced across it. The main line of retreat for the men on the plateau was lost. As men fell back to their horses for a scattered retreat into the foothills, Grant ordered his British artillerymen to abandon their field guns. One battery of three guns escaped, but nine were captured, most of them without even having breech blocks removed. Soon afterwards, the brigade's field ambulance section was cut off and the Turks captured four horse-drawn ambulances with a number of drivers and wounded.

Meanwhile, the brigade made a nightmarish retreat across a jagged series of limestone

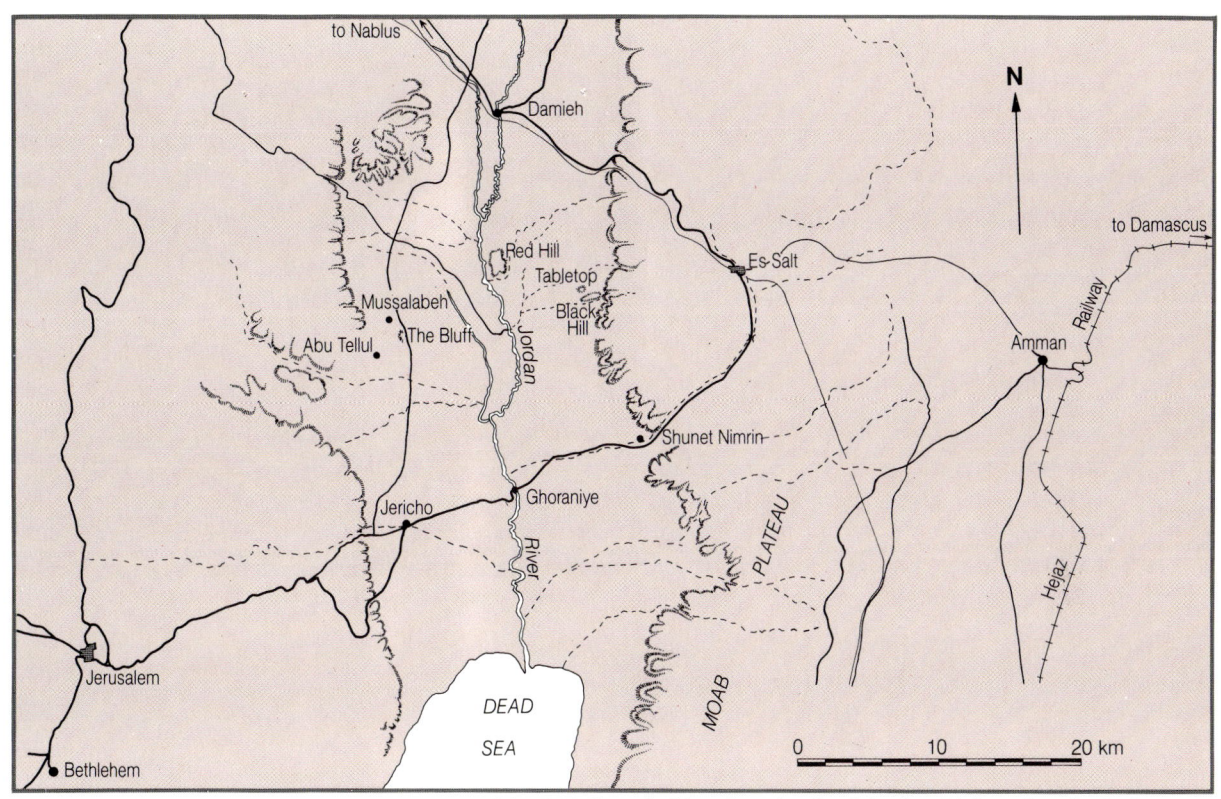

The raids on Amman and Es Salt in March and April 1918 resulted in exhausting, hard-fought withdrawals to the Jordan.

ridges. "I shall never forget the horror of that ride," said Trooper Alf Hird of the machine-gun squadron, "slipping, sliding, crawling from ledge to ledge. A slip and a horse would topple over and fall for perhaps a hundred feet. At times, we had to force them to drop from ledge to ledge like goats. Here and there, one would miss a ledge and that was the end of that particular horse."

At last, Grant managed to consolidate his brigade along a second goat track from Es Salt. This was now the only chance of escape for the three brigades now engaged on the plateau. But General Liman von Sanders, who had taken over command of the Turkish forces when von Falkenhayn and von Kress returned to Germany in March, made a crucial mistake. Instead of concentrating all his men on the defenders of this lifeline, he sent some units up the main Damieh Track to Es Salt.

In the quaint hill town clinging to steep slopes at the head of its valley, a grim siege was developing. The 1st and 2nd Brigades had joined the 3rd. The Turks were counter-attacking from Amman, and a large force was advancing up the Damieh track. Yeomanry had ridden to support the infantry attack on Shunet Nimrin but were blocked by Turks. No Arab support had appeared – apart from a few locals who vanished like mountain mists when the fighting began. And in the valley, the light-horsemen holding open the goat track were waging a desperate battle.

A second night passed without sleep, men on the plateau almost freezing, men in the valley seriously short of water. The third day of the action saw serious fighting above and below. On a little natural fortress called Table Top defending the goat track, men of the 4th Light Horse beat back Turkish attacks until their ammunition and grenades were exhausted, then bombarded the enemy with rocks before retreating. That night, the regiment was reinforced by a squadron of the 12th Light Horse and a troop of Yeomanry on neighbouring Black Hill, which became a

Victorious troops wait their turn to water their horses at Es Salt. The victory was short-lived, however, and the subsequent withdrawal was encumbered by fleeing Christian civilians.

strongpoint to keep the goat track open.

Next afternoon, May 3, Allenby drove to Chauvel's headquarters in the Jordan Valley and grimly studied the situation. He was reluctant to admit failure but realistic about his chances of success. As he told Chauvel, "I can't lose half my mounted troops." A general retirement was ordered.

That evening, a disciplined withdrawal began from Es Salt, walking wounded and Christian civilian refugees stumbling down the appalling little track. Then the brigades followed, and many men lifted struggling women and children into their saddles. In the darkness, a trooper was heard arguing with an old man begging a ride for his wife: "She's fallen off twice, and I'm tired of her. Why didn't you teach her to ride? However, up she goes for the last time."

The light-horsemen brought more than 600 Turkish prisoners with them, leaving only two seriously wounded men in the Turkish hospital. The rearguard slipped away at 3.45 the following morning, amused to see a major attack on the positions they had just left. "The Turks were at liberty to attack their own deserted hills to their hearts content," an officer commented.

All that day, the reinforced 4th Brigade fought desperately to hold their ground while men, women, children, horses and camels streamed down the goat track. By 10 a.m. the enemy were on three sides of the 4th Regiment on Black Hill and Grant had one position held by headquarters grooms and batmen. But with more reinforcements, the brigade hung on until the Es Salt rearguard had passed down the track. Then, after nightfall, they withdrew, again without the Turks knowing. Again, the light-horsemen watched an attack on their just-abandoned positions.

Bone-dry, bone-weary light-horsemen and infantry straggled back across the Jordan. "I have never seen a large body of men more exhausted than these men were after that backsheesh Es Salt stunt," said Trooper Chook Fowler. "Most of the men were too exhausted to erect a sun shelter, and were found sleeping in the very hot sun." Men and horses were issued with their first ration of food and forage in five days. Then came the reckoning of this ill-advised action. The Light

The Greek monastery built into the cliff face of the Mount of Temptation shimmers in the blistering heat of the Jordan Valley summer.

Horse had lost 50 killed, 278 wounded and 37 missing. But to some military minds, far more appalling than these casualties was the loss of the nine field guns. The British army had always been obsessive about losing guns, and while nothing was said or written, Grant was held responsible. Next in line for the brigade command was Colonel Bourchier of the 4th Regiment, who had played a distinguished role in holding the escape route. His star, brightened by Beersheba, was on the rise.

Now a new enemy appeared, the Jordan Valley summer. Temperatures had risen sharply through spring, and the valley mud had dried to a fine, cement-like powder that rose in choking clouds, "painting everything within reach a loathsome putty colour," a trooper wrote. "On a calm day the man riding in front half a horse's length away would be blotted from view." The heat was legendary. Apart from monks in the monastery clinging to the cliff-like Mount of Temptation, the lighthorsemen became the first Europeans to pass a summer in the valley. Even the Bedouin and many local Arabs left the area. Shade temperatures were often claimed to reach 54 degrees Celsius. But while a senior medical officer reported the highest shade temperature as 45.5 degrees, he also quoted bell tents in which the temperature reached 52 degrees. Another medical officer noted that the coolest part of a hospital marquee reached 56 degrees. Temperatures declined only a few degrees at night, and men without mosquito nets, who had to wrap themselves in blankets to avoid mosquito bites, woke in the morning lying in puddles of sweat.

Besides mosquitoes, there were lice, flies, centipedes and scorpions. The scorpions – giants of over 15 centimetres – often gathered under ground sheets. A trooper wrote, "At night they would crawl on or under what passed for one's pillow. When lying awake they could be heard crackling slightly as they walked, due perhaps to the jointed armour of their remarkably large bodies."

Bites of the scorpions and centipedes were extremely painful, but mosquito bites were more deadly. They spread malaria. Even though men evacuated with the disease never accounted for more than 1.5 per cent of the corps at any given time, one man in four would contract the disease that year, and 101 would die from it.

Like everyone else, the British official correspondent hated the Jordan Valley. "It was dreadfully oppressive," he said, "and I never came out of it without a violent headache." He also commented: "It was somewhat of a relief from the trials of the climate when the enemy decided to take action." There were air raids, long-range artillery bombardment and a few attempts to break the British line. Now, in mid-summer, the enemy launched a major attack on Australian positions, spearheaded by German infantrymen of the Asia Korps. It was intended as a showpiece action, a demonstration to the Turks of how it should be done.

A little north of Jericho, the Light Horse held a group of trench systems and redoubts based on two rocky outcrops at Abu Tellul and Mussalabeh. Each post was trenched and wired separately, with its own stores of food and munitions, including hand grenades and rifle grenades. Water was stored in petrol tins and empty beer bottles. On the night of July 13, the 1st Light Horse Brigade held the group of posts and were starting to enjoy a beer ration after a day of brutal heat. The 1st Regiment was in reserve.

At 3:30 a.m. the attack came – three battalions of German infantry, the 702nd, the 703rd and the 11th Jaegers, supported by the crack Turkish 24th Division. A trooper of the 3rd Light Horse Regiment wrote: "Their

Troopers bivouac among the rocks at the Mussalabeh outpost. This knoll, which marked the northern point of British occupation on the western side of the Jordan Valley, was the scene of two strong enemy attacks.

Lines of dummy horses were erected in the Jordan Valley as part of a plan to trick the enemy into believing there was still a concentration of forces there. Meanwhile, the Desert Mounted Corps assembled on the coast.

bravery, almost foolhardy, carried some of these Germans blindly to within a few feet of barbed and entrenched posts where they would fling themselves down and start shooting, if they got the time to do so, with their neat and handy looking automatic rifles. Their fury and disregard of normal care was most impressive." This cool and clinical observation of the attack captures the mood of the Australians. They were at last fighting Germans, the "real" enemy of that "real" and distant war. They fought with a terrible calmness and precision.

At dawn, the Germans took one post, only when every light-horseman was dead or wounded. The remaining nine posts were completely surrounded by German troops. One, on a rocky outcrop called the Bluff, held out with only three men unwounded.

Like Chauvel at Romani, Brigadier-General Cox waited until daylight gave him the whole picture. Then he turned to Lieutenant-Colonel C.H. Granville of the waiting 1st Regiment and said simply, "Get to them, Granny!" The men of the 1st launched a superb bayonet charge, cheered on by their mates in the besieged posts. They drove the startled Germans off Abu Tellul into a crucible of crossfire from the surrounding Australian positions, where, said one trooper, "they ran about like a lot of mad rabbits."

Successive attacks on the Bluff and the other posts broke the German attack. Hundreds of dead were scattered outside the wire; 105 bodies lay inside the positions. The Australians took 425 prisoners, 358 of them German, and lost 23 dead and 46 wounded. In five and a half hours, they had fired 69,000 rounds of ammunition.

It was noted that some of the German prisoners were falling-down drunk. They had captured some of the 1st Brigade's beer ration. Others were "frantic with thirst" when captured. Recalled a trooper: "So pleased were they at getting all the water they needed and being treated in a civilized way that they cheered us from the trucks as they left for prison camps." One of the prisoners, a man of the 702nd Battalion, later wrote: "We had very heavy losses and I should imagine that the Asia Korps has practically ceased to exist." In that estimate, he was correct. What was more, the last enemy offensive of the entire Palestine campaign was broken.

Although the summer had passed its awful peak, the light-horsemen continued to curse the valley until, regiment by regiment, they began to slip away. They spelled at Solomon's Pools near Bethlehem, some men swimming while others shot water snakes. They strolled around Jerusalem in small, officer-led parties. Then, instead of going back to the valley, they rode west, always by night, towards the coast with its beaches and gentle Mediterranean surf. "Daily we would strip off and give the horses a treat," recalled a trooper, "Men freed of their clothing and the horse with nothing except rider and bridle, looking like a grecian frieze, washed off months of travail and recreated themselves afresh." Soon, all of the Australian Mounted Division had been smuggled eastwards, to camp hidden among olive groves and orange orchards near Ludd.

Meanwhile, back in the Jordan Valley, curious things were happening. An officer noted: "During daylight hours, empty vehicles poured down from Jerusalem along roads visible to the Turks on the east of Jordan, and branches of trees were towed along the valley northwards, creating dust to simulate movement of troops, then dummy horses were rigged up on regular lines – bags of grass with bushes for tails – anything to create shadows of horses." Great lines of empty bell tents shone in the fierce sunlight. Massed ranks of infantry marched down into the valley every day, but had vanished by the next morning. The men of the Anzac Division watched it all and wondered. Then they shrugged and went about their chores, living members of a great ghost army of the valley, part of the most fabulous hoax in military history.

THE NEW MACHINES OF WAR

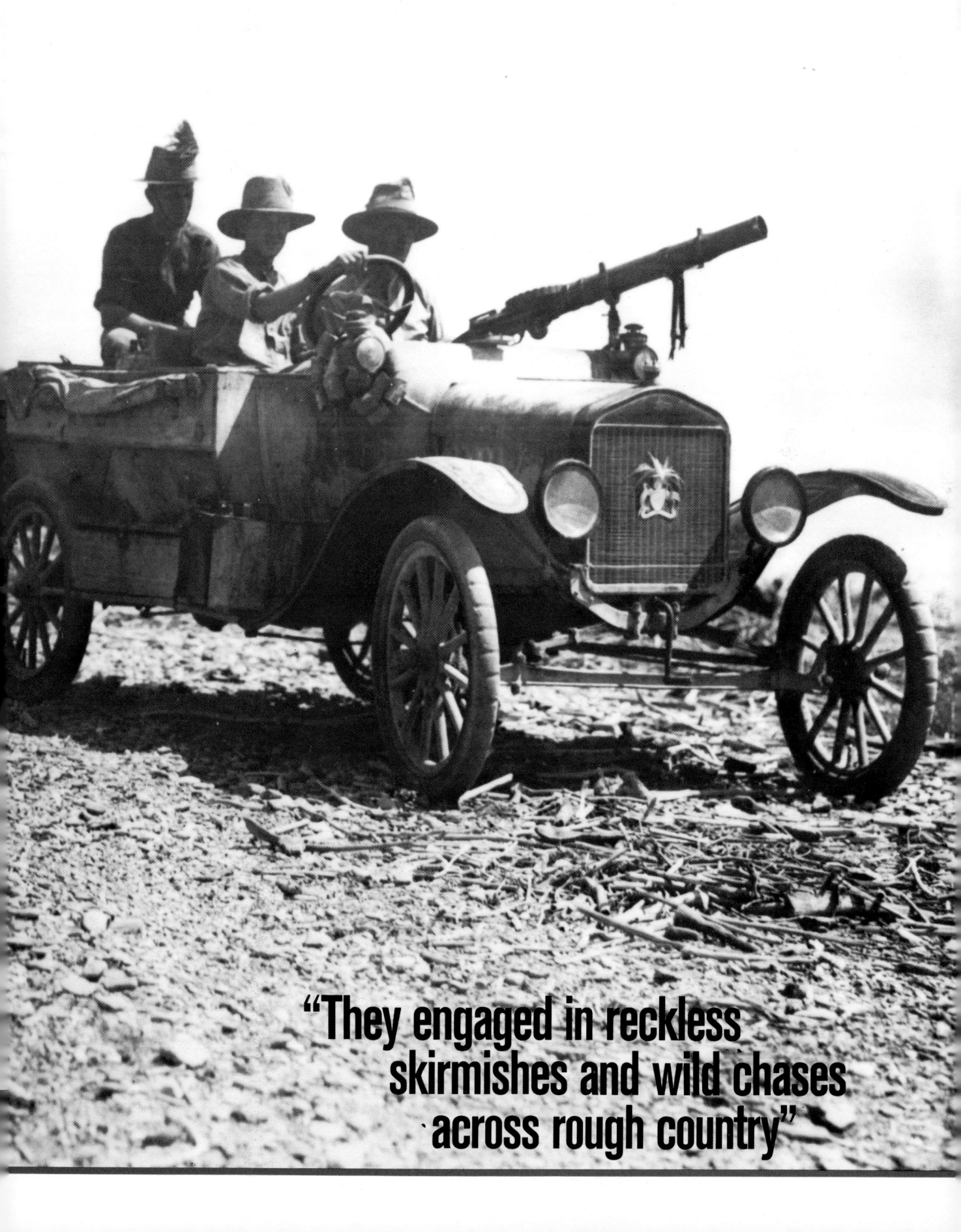

No. 1 Australian Light Car Patrol returns from the Jordan Valley to the Dead Sea post.

"They engaged in reckless skirmishes and wild chases across rough country"

A DIFFERENT KIND OF HORSEPOWER

Even before the war's end, there were signs that the days of cavalry were numbered and that, in future, soldiers would not be mounted on horses but would ride on and in machines. The bicycle, the motor cycle, the armoured car, the tank, the aeroplane — all were used in World War I, with varying degrees of effectiveness, and many light-horsemen were keen to try out these new machines of war, even though it meant giving up their trusty walers.

Much admired were the 1st Australian Light Car Patrol, in their Model T Fords armed with Lewis machine-guns. Together with the British 7th Light Car Patrol, they were used in Palestine for reconnaissance and other operations, often well in advance to the mounted troops, where they engaged in reckless skirmishes and wild chases across rough country. They became heroes in the eyes of the Light Horse.

Light-horsemen were also eager recruits for the Australian Flying Corps, which was formed in 1915 as part of the Australian Imperial Force — that is, the army — though tactically they were part of the British Royal Flying Corps. No. 1 Squadron, which served in Sinai and Palestine, was the most renowned of the AFC's four squadrons. In the inferior aircraft with which they were equipped during the Sinai campaign, they managed to hold their own against the German airmen. Later, equipped with Bristol Fighters, they were more than a match for the Germans and in one eight-week period in 1918 accounted for all 15 enemy aircraft destroyed on the Palestine front.

Least effective of the fighting machines used in Palestine were the six British tanks, one of which came to a fiery end amid doomed Australian cameleers at the second battle of Gaza. But whatever the relative effectiveness of the vehicles and aircraft used in World War I, it was clear that machines would provide the horsepower in future wars.

A Light Horse dispatch rider sets off on his motor cycle with a cargo of carrier pigeons. Despite Allenby's initial objections, light-horsemen were allowed to dress in shirtsleeves and slacks instead of heavy riding gear in the heat of the Jordan Valley.

No. 1 Australian Light Car Patrol lines up at Aleppo railway station. Driving Ford cars mounted with Lewis machine-guns, the Light Car Patrol constantly engaged in sporting fights against great odds.

Light-horsemen impatient to see action abandoned their horses in Egypt to join the Cyclist Battalion in France, led by former Light Horse major Jack Hindhaugh.

Armoured Rolls-Royce cars operating with the Australian Light Horse make a mid-desert halt in the Jordan Valley.

Men of the Light Car Patrol in Egypt push and heave to extricate one of their armoured cars from a patch of soft sand.

Troopers examine the remains of a British tank destroyed in the Battle of Gaza. It was later used by the enemy as a redoubt.

Four bombs hang from each lower wing of an RE8 aircraft, used by the Australian Flying Corps in Sinai.

Puffs of smoke mark the bomb blasts of an air raid on Amman airfield and railway station in June 1918. By this time the Australian Flying Corps, which attracted many recruits from the Light Horse, were flying the faster Bristol Fighter.

Captain Ross Smith, a former Light Horse sergeant, sits at the controls of a Bristol Fighter while his gunner mans a twin Lewis gun. Smith later commanded a Handley-Page bomber in which he made the first flight from Cairo to Calcutta. Right: Effects of Allied bombing—a truck lies wrecked across the railway track.

A Bristol Fighter—dubbed "the Yellow Peril" by the Germans—sets out on a reconnaissance mission over Aleppo in Syria. The billets of the 10th Wing of the AFC are in the background.

Two Light Horse officers and their Arab companion stand beside the skeleton of a German plane brought down near Aleppo.

5

THE GREAT RIDE

By a clever hoax, Allenby deceived the Turks into expecting an attack from the Jordan flank, then began the Great Ride up the coast. The Light Horse, now armed as cavalry, raced for Damascus, snatching the prize from Lawrence of Arabia.

No general with any battle experience expects his plans to go perfectly. He sits at his headquarters or stands on his hill and watches the awful chess game unfolding, hour by hour. His opponent behaves unpredictably, his own moves are fumbled by the numberless fibres of communication between his brain and the tens of thousands of pieces under his command. He plans perfection, yet, in the end, he is grateful for anything that grants him victory. But, in September 1918, General Allenby watched his plan to defeat the Turks in Palestine become a perfect reality. Its success exceeded all sane levels of expectation—both in scale and in time. He captured 650 kilometres of enemy territory in scarcely six weeks. He had been prepared for 30,000 casualties and gained his victory with less than 5,000. And all this after completely rebuilding his army in six months.

In March and April he had sent 60,000 men to France—two complete divisions, 22 battalions, five batteries of artillery and five machine-gun companies. Of the Indian troops who replaced them, two divisions of seasoned infantry came from Mesopotamia, but the remaining 22 battalions were, in Lloyd George's words, "largely made up of recruits who had

From the sketchbook of George Lambert.

done no musketry." Many of their officers could not even speak Hindustani. So intensive training began, and each new brigade would go into action with one battalion of British Tommies.

The Indian cavalry who replaced the Yeomanry were a great success with the Light Horse. They rode Australian walers and immediately impressed the Australians with their consummate horsemanship. A trooper summed it up: "We broke horses, they trained them." In their turn, the Indians revered the Light Horse as proved masters of mounted warfare. The foundation was laid for a remarkable working relationship.

The Camel Corps was marched out of the Jordan Valley and disbanded; the Englishmen went to France and the Australians traded in their camels for horses. They were then given Light Horse drill and became the 14th and 15th Regiments, core of a new 5th Light Horse Brigade. In an interesting development, the third regiment of the brigade was the Regiment Mixte de Marche de Palestine et Syrie—two squadrons of French Chasseurs d'Afrique and one of Spahis. A black cavalryman in a blue and red uniform riding a grey horse was a most unusual light-horseman, but he symbolised the pragmatism of Allenby and Chauvel as they prepared for the final campaign.

Another transformation was taking place on the coast among the olive and orange groves. The nine regiments of the Australian Mounted Division had asked to be issued with swords. The request was granted, and they were given a hectic three weeks of cavalry training with the standard British thrust sword, a superb weapon with a moulded grip, basket hilt, and slender 89-centimetre blade. A trooper commented: "They taught us to turn your wrist over and lock your elbow for the charge. They reckoned that the thrust sword at arm's length could out-reach a lance held at the couch, by a couple of inches. That cheered us up quite a bit, until we wondered what happened if your sword went more than a couple of inches through the bloke who had the lance!"

Light-horsemen trained with bags of straw slung from wooden gallows-frames and, unofficially, staged hair-raising sword fights on horseback and on foot. They were issued with the long cavalry-pattern rifle buckets for their .303s, slung from the offside of the saddle, and cavalry-pattern horseshoe cases with attached sword frogs slung at the near side. Then they posed for one another's box cameras among the olive trees at Ludd, showing off their new toys, scarcely aware that they were now Light Horse only in name. They had become cavalry, about to play a key role in the most remarkable cavalry campaign in the history of warfare.

Allenby was now opposing General Liman von Sanders, who had commanded the defence of Gallipoli. Von Sanders was a talented officer who, unlike von Falkenhayn, understood the Turks. But he inherited a demoralised, appallingly neglected and underfed force. Eight of his ten divisions had been in the line without relief for six months and were losing 1,000 men a month through desertion alone. The British now outnumbered von Sanders's Palestine armies by more than two to one. Despite all this, the man who had denied Britain, France, Australia and New Zealand anything more than a precarious toehold on the Gallipoli Peninsula was still a formidable opponent. Yet he was about to be outsmarted and outmanoeuvred on a scale rarely seen in warfare. Allenby was preparing to play his old left-hand, right-hand, feint and knockout strategy, so effectively set up by the two strikes across the Jordan.

The decoy activity in the Jordan Valley was continuing—empty camps, lines of dummy horses, dust, new bridges, troops marching into the valley by day and being trucked out again by night. A dummy headquarters had been set up in the Hotel Fast at Jerusalem—complete with wireless station on the roof and sign-written doors. Officers who had rented houses for the summer on the coast told landlords they would need them for the winter. And a "Great Horse Show" and race meeting at a small town near Jaffa was advertised for September 19. This effectively announced that the district was a dead sector and made it clear that the hundreds of army horses taking part in the events would not be needed for major action near that date. On September 19, virtually the entire population of Jaffa turned out in one long procession to see the grand spectacle. As they waited for the Horse Show That Never Was, the Desert Mounted Corps was setting out on what came to be called the Great Ride.

So tight was the security for the offensive that Allenby did not trust the plan to his own divisional commanders until two days before the advance. On the morning of September 17, Chauvel, Hodgson and the other brigadiers and commanding officers of the Australian Mounted Division gathered in the mess tent at divisional headquarters. Allenby greeted each of the 30-odd men by name, then began what one of them called a terse and soldierly address. "I have come, gentlemen, to wish you good luck, and to tell you that my impression is that you are on the eve of a great victory. Everything depends – well, perhaps not everything, but nearly everything – on the secrecy, rapidity and accuracy of the cavalry movement."

Allenby went on to sketch the strategic situation – the Turks entrenched across Palestine from the sea to the Hejaz Railway, expecting an attack towards Damascus in the Jordan sector, and unaware of the concentration of infantry and cavalry near the coast. He told his commanders how he planned to bombard the Turkish line just before dawn on the 19th, destroy their communications with aerial strikes, smash a gap with the infantry, then send his cavalry through the gap to spear northwards up the coast behind the enemy lines. They would cut in behind the Turkish Seventh and Eighth Armies and trap them in the Samarian Hills, pressed by the advancing infantry, battered by aerial attack. Allenby finished: "You have trained strenuously and devotedly at a time when you should have been enjoying a well-earned rest, after your long and trying summer in the Jordan Valley; but I hope and feel confident that you are at last about to reap the reward of you devotion."

General Hodgson then held a conference detailing the role of the various divisions. The 4th and 5th Divisions of Indian Cavalry and Yeomanry would lead off to the north, the 4th striking towards von Sanders's headquarters town of Nazareth while the 5th cut through a pass to the Esdraelon Plain near Megiddo, the Biblical Armageddon. The Light Horse would follow, holding the vital pass and aiming for Jenin, a major Turkish centre and key point on the escape route from Nablus. Nothing was put in writing, apart from the notes made by each officer. And even these were later destroyed.

The security precautions may have seemed a bit overdone, but they worked perfectly. A German map prepared on September 17 and issued the day before the attack showed exactly what Allenby wanted the Turks to believe – that "no essential change had taken place in the distribution of the British forces." Only the 5th Cavalry was shown on the coastal flank. The Australian Mounted Division and the 4th Division appeared with the Anzacs in the Jordan Valley, and Chauvel's headquarters were shown in their old position on the Jericho road.

At sunset the following day among the olive groves, the brigades loaded their horses with three days' food, an extra water bottle slung on the saddle, and extra bandolier around the neck. All surplus equipment had been discarded in huge dumps, much of it never to be seen again. Then the troopers mounted and set off in the deepening dusk, freed from the four-kilogram weight of .303 rifle across the shoulder, occasionally patting the butt protruding from its bucket close behind the right hand. One recalled, "I felt unarmed. As though I was heading off on a muster. I never thought I'd miss that bloody weight on my back." They moved to position in the gigantic queue, ready for the next day's advance, and slept by their horses – their last night's sleep for many days. That night, an Indian soldier, a devout Moslem, deserted to the Turks and tried to warn them of the coming attack. It was too late.

At 4:30 a.m., as dawn was breaking behind the Judaean Hills, 350 guns launched a preliminary 15-minute bombardment which then

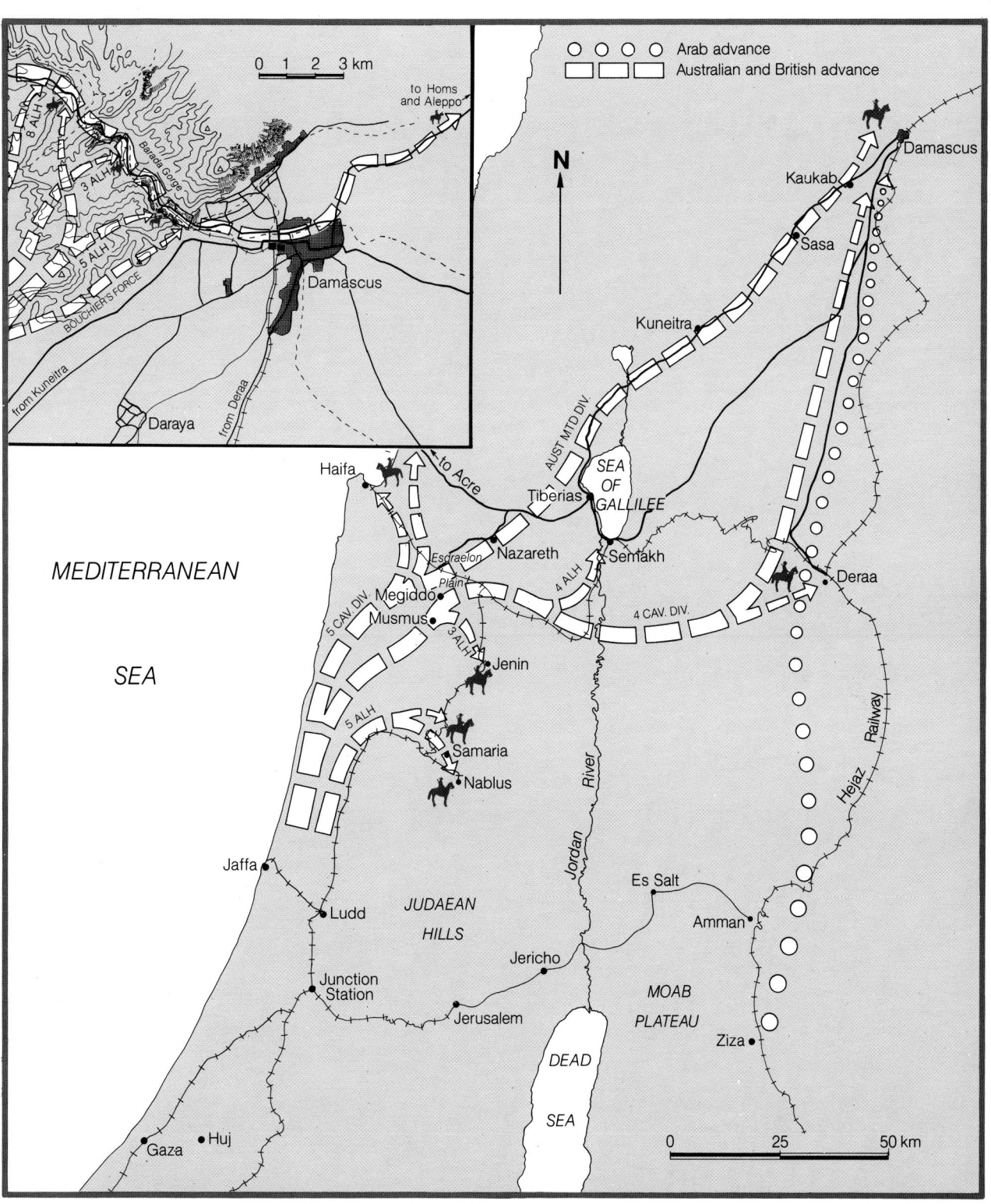

Allenby's plan for the defeat of the Turks in Palestine called for a swift and unexpected cavalry thrust up the coast and on to Damascus. At the same time (not shown on the map) the Anzac Mounted Division struck eastward from the Jordan Valley to Es Salt and Amman.

A Bristol Fighter of No. 1 Squadron, Australian Flying Corps, prepares to take off on a reconnaissance flight over Palestine. Australian fliers made 234 reconnaissances and 150 bombing raids between July and October 1918.

rolled back ahead of the infantry as they swarmed forward. Within an hour they had broken the Turkish line. The 4th and 5th Cavalry Divisions started off, followed by the Australian Mounted, led by the 3rd Light Horse Brigade with the 10th Regiment as vanguard. Lieutenant-Colonel A.C. Olden, temporarily commanding the regiment, led his men through the gap while infantry and engineers still rounded up prisoners and cleared away the debris of the bombardment. "They greeted our men with cheers and many cries of 'Good luck,'" Olden recalled, "which were heartily responded to by 'Same to you! We'll meet you in Damascus!'"

The vanguard rode all day and by 9:30 a.m. on September 20 were coming through the Musmus Pass, 48 kilometres behind the Turkish front line. Recalled Olden: "From here across the plain one could see Nazareth nestling in the opposite hills, and British and Indian Cavalry of the 4th Division working their way towards it." Chauvel wrote to his wife: "I have had a glorious time. We have done a regular Jeb Stuart ride." He went on to say that they were overlooking the plain of Armageddon, "which is still strewn with Turkish dead 'harpooned' by my Indian cavalry early this morning. . . .We are fighting what I sincerely hope will be the last 'Battle of Armageddon'."

The men of the Light Horse vanguard were "filled with admiration and delight" at the success of the Indian horsemen on their cherished walers. Now, in Olden's words, "they waited for the word to strike their first real blow of the battle." It came later that day. Aerial reconnaissance showed large bodies of Turks retreating on Jenin, a key road and rail junction and supply depot, 18 kilometres south-east.

At 4:35 p.m., five minutes after receiving orders to take Jenin, the 9th and 10th Regiments moved off down the Esdraelon Plain at the trot, riding 30 abreast. Apart from the holes made by land crabs and the countless stinging insects, it was perfect cavalry country – flat, featureless and hard-packed. The leading 10th Regiment broke to a canter as Jenin came into view at the foot of the plain. They drew away from the 9th, to cover almost 18 kilometres in 70 minutes.

Sighting a large body of enemy troops "taking it easy near an olive grove," Lieutenant P.W. Doig formed up his troop riding as flank guard and charged with drawn swords. After a brief fight, with a few Turkish soldiers wounded, the handful of Australians took 1,900 prisoners.

Groups of light-horsemen cut all roads from

A trooper surveys the scene at Jenin on the morning after its capture by the 3rd Light Horse Brigade. In the days that followed, roads out of Jenin were thronged with Arabs carrying looted war material.

Jenin; then a single squadron charged a huge mass of Turks and Germans forming up in the town. The phalanx of yelling Australians galloping out of the sunset with unwavering swords shocked another 3,000 troops into surrender. A trooper noted: "Officers among the prisoners had no idea their front line had been broken." Apart from some sniping by small groups of German diehards, the battle was over.

By now it was dark and Jenin had become what Chauvel's biographer, A.J. Hill, called "a kind of military witches' carnival." Dumps of stores, the railway station and a couple of dozen aircraft were ablaze, lighting a scene of total chaos as men, women and children fought for the contents of buildings and vehicles, screaming "Arab! Arab!", seen as "the password with the 'Inglese' to permit them to rob and pillage," according to Colonel Olden. The password did not impress the light-horsemen, but even shots fired over the looters' heads failed to stop them. The men of the 10th rescued a wagon loaded with £250,000 worth of bullion.

With moonrise, parties of light-horsemen went out to intercept Turks retreating down the Nablus road. Lieutenant R.R.W. Patterson, with 23 men and two machine-guns, met a column marching down from the hills, halted them with a burst of fire over their heads, and persuaded them to surrender, claiming that he was supported by a large force. The 24 Australians captured 2,800 troops and four field guns.

By the next day the 10th Light Horse and its machine-gunners had captured 8,107 prisoners, including several divisional commanders with their staffs and many officers of high rank. General Hodgson commented: "I suppose never before in the history of the world has such a number of prisoners been taken by so small a force as one regiment." The record would be broken within 11 days.

Meanwhile, the 4th Brigade was mustering the growing horde of prisoners while the brand new 5th Brigade cut the railway line north of Samaria and struck at Nablus. Their advance had not been without teething troubles. The brigade major was a British permanent officer of the Indian army. He considered this type of campaigning "a damn nuisance" and was eventually sent back to the sick lines as "having had a severe fall from his horse." Captain Rex Hall replaced the major and soon found himself accepting the surrender of Nablus from the civic authorities. "I rode to the Town Hall where I was handed the keys of the city. They were very heavy and I took them away spread across the pommel of my saddle. Enemy were popping off rifles in the streets, and changing into civilian clothes to avoid capture." Captain Hall was clearly philosophical about this. Fewer prisoners to handle. He was less philosophical about the French cavalrymen riding with the brigade. They were looting meat, vegetables and grain, with the approval of their officers. Said Captain Hall: "Without their customary supply of coffee and wine, both of which had been left behind with our wheeled vehicles, this regiment became most difficult."

Despite its problems, the 5th Brigade scooped up 3,726 prisoners in four days and pushed the remnants of the Seventh and Eight Turkish Armies towards the west. British and Australian airmen located one huge column heading along a gorge towards the Jordan. In historian Henry Gullett's chilling description, "Descending to within a few hundred feet of their helpless quarry, the airmen quickly smashed up the leading vehicles and choked the gorge. Then flying up and down the doomed, chaotic train of motors, guns and horse transport, through which surged thousands of distracted troops, the pilots and observers continued their terrible work with both bombs and machine guns."

While the attack was in progress, the 5th Light Horse Brigade appeared on the hills to both sides, their flashing swords offering surrender from the hell of the gorge. Major Oliver Hogue of the 14th Regiment wrote: "Most of us had seen death and slaughter before. Some of us had four years of warfare behind us. But none of us will forget the day we rode through "The Valley of Death'." Within a week he would help create another, more hideous Valley of Death.

As the first retreating Turkish troops came in sight of the Jordan, the waiting Anzacs rode to block them from the fords. Only a few hundred men managed to straggle across. In the first three days of the Great Ride, 15,000 prisoners had been taken. The Turkish Seventh and Eighth Armies had virtually ceased to exist.

Now, while Chauvel sent his horsemen against Haifa and Acre on the coast and Tiberias and Semakh on the Sea of Galilee, the Anzacs crossed the Jordan and rode for Es Salt and Amman. This was their third strike across the Jordan, the third time they had been promised Arab support. But this time, Lawrence and his Arabs came good. They would strike at Deraa, a railway junction 70 kilometres north of Amman, almost cutting off the Turkish Fourth Army and massacring its stragglers. To the south, the Anzacs took Es Salt and moved on Amman from the north and west. After a short, ugly little battle in which 2,500 of the Turkish rearguard were captured, Australians and New Zealanders raced each other in a dead heat to the citadel of the town. Some of the lighthorsemen suffered a bitter disappointment when, after working for hours to open a locked safe from the Amman railway station, they found it packed with thousands of tickets.

The only body of Turkish resistance east of the Jordan was now the 5,000-man garrison of Maan, trying to retreat towards Amman and harried by a huge force of Bedouin of the Beni Sakr tribe. Aircraft sighted the Turks at Ziza, dug in behind circular earthworks and surrounded by 10,000 Arabs. With two squadrons of his 5th Light Horse Regiment, Lieutenant-Colonel Donald Cameron rode to Ziza and was told that the Turkish commander wished to surrender but was afraid to do so. "He maintained that my small force was not strong enough to protect his men from the Bedouin if the garrison laid down its arms," Cameron later recounted.

Looking at the beleaguered Turks, the 10,000 blood-thirsting Arabs and his own men, Cameron was forced to agree. One of his officers sent to explain the situation returned with the written message: "To the O.C. British Forces, Colonel Cameron – I hereby surrender unconditionally all my force, guns, ammunition, stores etc. and in so doing claim your protection for the safety of my soldiers, wounded and sick. Signed at Ziza, 29th September, 1918. Bey Wahaby, Commandant."

Waiting for reinforcements, Cameron urged the Turks to man all their defences if he could not join them by nightfall and told the Arabs that if they attacked the Turks, he would attack

Gazing over the Sea of Galilee, three members of the 8th Light Horse Regimental Signal Station wait beside their heliograph on the pier at Tiberias. Tiberias was captured by the 8th and 12th Regiments on September 25, 1918.

them. But then at last the 7th Light Horse arrived at the gallop. Their commanding officer, Lieutenant J.D. Richardson, reported: "The vulture appearance of the Arabs, who were willing that we should do the fighting, and they the looting, will never be forgotten."

Now General Chaytor rode up, and the irate Bey Wahaby asked permission to attack the Arabs. Chaytor calmed Wahaby and took him to Amman, assuring him that his men were in good hands. This was indeed true, because by now Brigadier-General Ryrie had arrived. He approached the problem with the shrewdness of the politician he was and the pugnacity of the boxer he had been. Accompanied by two sheikhs of the Beni Sakr, he led the slim band of light-horsemen into the Turkish position at the gallop. Then, once inside, he told the sheikhs that, if their warriors attacked, they would be immediately shot. This clear message was relayed to the waiting Arabs, and then the 600-odd light-horsemen and the 5,000 Turks settled down to one of the strangest nights of comradeship in the history of warfare. In Gullett's words, "They gathered about the same fires, exchanging their food, making chappaties together, and by many signs expressing reciprocal respect and admiration." When Arabs prowled too close, Turkish sentries reacted with bursts of machine-gun and rifle fire, bringing appreciative roars of laughter from the Australians and shouts of "Go on, Jacko! Give it to the blighters!"

In the morning, the New Zealand Brigade arrived and the Turks happily laid down their arms and marched off to Amman. This ended the remarkable Ziza incident – and brought the Anzacs, tally of prisoners to 10,300 in nine days.

West of the Jordan, Haifa and Acre had been taken easily. But in Galilee, resistance was tougher. Von Sanders, who had escaped from Nazareth in his pyjamas as British and Indian troops entered the town, had tried to organize lines of defence, often issuing orders that would never be delivered to units that had ceased to exist. But at Semakh, on the southern shore of the Sea of Galilee, he had personally ordered a last-ditch stand as he passed through. This small Arab village and railway settlement barred the main northern route between the waters of the giant lake and the flanking hills.

Before dawn on September 25, Brigadier-General Grant advanced towards Semakh with part of his 4th Light Horse Brigade, the 11th Regiment and part of the 12th. Grant knew that a few hundred enemy riflemen and machine-gunners were stationed around the railway buildings, which included a two-storey stone station — a ready-made fortress for the garrison. Grant had a reputation for decisive, almost impulsive action. Beersheba had been his triumph. Since then, the aborted charge at Wadi Sheria and the loss of the guns at Damieh had clouded that reputation — or, perhaps just as significantly, Grant's self-esteem. He sent his men forward without waiting for the 5th Brigade, which was moving up in support.

Trooper Chook Fowler, the nuggety little campaigner of the 12th Regiment, was drowsing as he rode through the cool pre-dawn. He had been droving prisoners for two days without sleep. As he dismounted at 7 p.m. the previous night, he had been told to move out in 45 minutes. He rode 80 kilometres by 1 a.m. to rejoin his regiment, and moved out with it at 2 a.m. "Riding along half asleep and still dark," he recalled, "suddenly the air was filled with the rattle of machine-gun and rifle fire. We stopped and were told that the 11th Regiment would form up on our left flank, ready to charge and capture Semakh, while we acted as moving targets for the enemy gunners. Many times we rode over and back again, with a stream of bullets flying around, but mostly overhead: we must have been closer to the enemy than they thought we were, to our great benefit. . . . Our horses knew what those bullets meant, and we had to work to control them. I know my pony stood on his hind legs many times, and tried to gallop away."

To the order "Charge the guns!", two squadrons of the 11th formed up with swords and spurred at the gun flashes. They quickly disposed of a nest of German machine-gunners, then came under fire from the railway buildings a kilometre and a half away, and charged towards them across the moonlit, dry-grassed flats. At about 800 metres range, with men and horses going down, one squadron veered left to take cover in the huts of the village, while the second swung right, flanking the station.

Men of both squadrons made a dismounted bayonet charge, which was halted by heavy rifle and machine-gun fire from German and Turkish troops in railway carriages and trucks, as well as from the main force in the stone buildings. A squadron of the 12th Light Horse Regiment and machine-gunners galloped in from the left and raked the enemy positions. As day broke, the men of the 11th charged the station complex under this covering fire. One squadron battled among the rolling stock, while their mates crashed into the station building and waged an ugly bayonet fight through its rooms and up its narrow staircase.

With daylight, 15 light-horsemen were dead and 70 wounded. Nearly 100 horses were killed or wounded, many of them scattered, stiff-legged, over the course of the charge. It was the costliest cavalry action of the offensive. But nearly 100 enemy troops had been killed — most of them German — and 365 were prisoners. The light-horsemen buried their dead in a neat little cemetery beside the Sea of Galilee, then headed north for Damascus.

Allenby had waited three days after the Great Ride had begun before he shared with Chauvel his plan to continue the advance to Damascus. It had been a characteristic exchange: "What about Damascus?" from Allenby; "Rather!" from Chauvel. The general who had been called a "sticky old frog" was enjoying his giant hops across Palestine. And now he prepared for the greatest hop of all.

On the evening of September 26, Chauvel ordered the Yeomanry and Indians of the 4th Division to try to cut off the Turkish Fourth Army at Deraa. If unsuccessful (which they were, arriving only in time to interrupt the Arab massacre of stragglers), they would move up the Hejaz Railway to Damascus. The Australian Mounted Division, followed by the 5th Cavalry, would skirt the Sea of Galilee, cross the Jordan at the northern end, then also strike straight for Damascus, destination of the retreating Turks and the last great enemy bastion. It was a gigantic race for the glittering prize of this most ancient of cities, "the Pearl of the Orient" as one Light Horse officer called it. The 4th Division faced a ride of 225 kilometres. The Light Horse started a day later with 145 kilometres to cover.

German rearguard machine-gunners made desperate stands at the Jordan and beyond, sometimes fighting to the death, often escaping by lorry at the last moment. An officer of the 3rd Brigade vanguard had high praise for their fortitude. However, he recalled that approaching Kuneitra the only rearguards were "grotesque little piles of stones strikingly resembling human heads and shoulders." The town was empty of enemy troops, and white flags fluttered everywhere. "Kuneitra looked like a Chinese laundry on Monday," said one trooper. But at Sasa, 29 kilometres south of Damascus, a massive rearguard of 1,200 Turks, 300 German machine-gunners and four field guns launched a night ambush on the 3rd Brigade spearhead. After a bitter, blind fight over appallingly rocky and treacherous ground, the enemy jumped into their lorries and could be heard rumbling away. A squadron of the 10th Light Horse mounted, spurred after them, and captured one lorry load.

Now, before dawn on September 30, a new vanguard took over. In an unusual move, Chauvel and Hodgson took the two regiments that had charged at Beersheba – the 4th and 12th Light Horse – and formed them into a strike force under the man who had led the charge, Lieutenant-Colonel Bourchier of the 4th. Grant and the remaining regiment of his brigade, the 11th, remained at Kuneitra "for the defence of communications."

"Bourchier's Force," as it was called, set a cracking pace, at first through narrow, rocky passes with snipers on both flanks. Then, at daylight, they struck out across a plain where last-ditch machine-gun posts were outflanked in a series of brilliant charges by advance patrols. A party of 200 infantry, mainly German, staged another ambush but were broken by a single troop who charged in from their left flank. Yet another rearguard of 300 infantry covering a retreating column was broken by one troop.

Bourchier was ordered to occupy Kaukab Ridge, a commanding height only 16 kilometres from Damascus. He reported: "When the advance guard was about one mile from Kaukab the retiring enemy's force about two miles in length was seen to be taking up a strong commanding position on a high ridge of hills near Kaukab." Bourchier's advance guard estimated the enemy force as "2500 infantry and cavalry and numerous machine guns." The colonel drew up his two regiments behind a ridge about 900 metres from the Turkish position. Under covering fire from two batteries of the Royal Horse Artillery, two squadrons of the 12th Light Horse would sweep in on the enemy's left, while two squadrons of the 4th Light Horse made a frontal attack. Two other squadrons would be held in reserve.

Again, men of the two Beersheba regiments would ride across a covering ridge to attack numerically superior forces in a formidable position. This time, they had to charge across a valley and up a slope. But now, they were carrying swords and they were charging a retreating enemy. Major Norman Rae was leading A Squadron of the 4th Regiment. "I moved them off with drawn swords in line and broke into a trot and then gallop," he recalled. "I never looked around but when I came down to top speed and sword at the 'charge', I could hear the noise behind me."

The four squadrons crashed down the stony hillside and up the facing slope in breathtaking style, the 4th avoiding two obstructive ravines without breaking formation. Trooper Fowler rode with the 12th. "We expected to go through heavy machine-gun fire. I heard someone yell as we galloped along, 'Why don't you fire, you

War artist George Lambert's oil painting of Barada Gorge shows men of the 5th Light Horse Brigade preparing to fire on the enemy from the rocky heights. Wrote Brigadier-General George Macarthur Onslow: "I turned eight machine-guns and every available rifle onto this mass of humanity — it was awful."

bastards?'" It was hard on the nerves, waiting for the blizzard of bullets, until the men realised that the 2,500 Turks were breaking and running, some into wooded country near by, while the mounted troops among them galloped for Damascus. Even a rearguard of 70 surrendered without firing a shot from their 12 machine-guns. Bourchier told the elated Major Rae, "The charge was like a drill manoeuvre."

As the charge had thundered across the valley, the Chasseurs d'Afrique and Spahis of the 5th Light Horse Brigade were striking out to the left – and probably encouraging the evacuation of Kaukab Ridge. They came in sight of a huge Turkish column retreating from Damascus and eventually scouted a position above the Barada Gorge. "What a sight met their eyes!" said Captain Hall, at last ready to forgive the foibles of his troublesome Frenchmen. "The Gorge is a deep ravine along which runs the Barada River (one of the rivers of Damascus), tree-lined and having the railway and road on its bank. Along the road was the column of fleeing Turks, a polyglot crowd; horses, cattle jinkers, and horse-drawn buggies carrying soldiers and civilians, men and women. Soon the French were shooting down at the column until they practically stopped all movement forward."

More men of the 5th Light Horse Brigade, and the 3rd, reached the gorge closer to the city. German machine-gunners on lorries ignored calls to surrender, and the light-horsemen opened fire, with rifles and machine-guns. Major Oliver Hogue, who had been appalled by the "Valley of Death" in Samaria, was among the officers who reluctantly ordered the bloodbath. Firing continued intermittently into the night, until the gorge was an obscene shambles of wrecked vehicles, dead and dying men, women, horses, cattle and camels. It would take 300 German prisoners a fortnight to clear the debris.

Meanwhile, Bourchier had handed the vanguard position back to the 3rd Brigade and joined them at the base of the foothills near the edge of the luxuriant gardens of Damascus. It was dusk on September 30. They had travelled 400 kilometres, according to the map, in 12 days. Many regiments had actually ridden nearly 650 kilometres. Under orders not to enter the city, the light-horsemen had a grandstand view as the Turks burnt stores and blew up their ammunition dumps. Far into the night, huge explosions reverberated among the surrounding hills and hurled trails of smoke across the sky. "Occasionally," said British correspondent W.T. Massey, "high up in the smoke clouds you could see two or three large shells burst like rockets. Small-arms ammunition was blown sky-high and burst like golden rain."

With first light, the 10th Light Horse headed the 3rd Brigade to skirt the city and intercept Turks escaping along the northern road to Homs and Aleppo. Riding along the Barada Gorge, they had to clear a trail through the carnage of the previous day and night, killing wounded animals and carrying wounded men to the banks of the river. Soon they reached the outskirts of Damascus and, across the Barada, could see thousands of Turkish soldiers milling around a massive, walled barracks. A few shots were fired at the Australians, but a feint charge sent the snipers scuttling for cover, and the vanguard continued at the canter until they came in sight of a huge crowd outside the Hall of Government on the opposite bank.

Major Olden, again second-in-command of the regiment, led his men across a bridge to investigate. He asked where the Governor was and, being told he was waiting in the hall above, dismounted and led two of his officers, with drawn revolvers, up a marble stairway. Inside a handsome chamber, recalled Olden, "a large gathering, clad in the glittering garb of eastern officialdom, stood, formed up in rows. Their general demeanour was quiet and dignified. Behind a table, in a high-backed gold and plush chair, sat a small man of distinguished appearance, wearing European clothes and a tarboosh." This was Emir Said, who told Olden that he had been installed as Governor before the Turkish commander fled the city the previous day and that he now surrendered Damascus to the "first of the British Army." He assured Major Olden that there would be no more shooting in the streets and wrote a document to commemorate the historic occasion.

With an Armenian colonel as guide, Olden left the Hall of Government and again led the 3rd Light Horse Brigade towards the Aleppo Road. "The march now assumed the aspect of a triumphal procession," he said, "the dense masses of people rapidly becoming hysterical in their manifestations of joy. They clung to the horses' necks, they kissed our men's stirrups, they showered confetti and rose water over them; they shouted, laughed, cried, sang and clapped hands. From the windows of high buildings, Moslem women, raising their dark veils, called out, 'Meit allo Wesahla! Meit allo Wesahla!' ('A hundred welcomes'). The cry was taken up and carried along the line of march in one continuous chant."

Olden obviously enjoyed the moment, his black Arab polo pony prancing through the tumultuous streets. It was a taste of triumph that few modern warriors had shared. But it was soon time to depart, and he led his men out of the city by 7 a.m. – two hours before the triumphant entry of Lawrence of Arabia in his white and gold robes, riding in a blue Rolls Royce. Lawrence would not let this trifling detail spoil his story when, eight years later, he wrote *The Seven Pillars of Wisdom*.

While Olden was still in the Hall of Government, General Hodgson, who knew nothing of his detour, ordered Bourchier to reconnoitre the city. The 4th Regiment's C Squadron, under Major J.C. Chanter, advanced through orchards and gardens under constant sniping. They found a huge mass of munitions and supplies at a railway station and, leaving a guard, advanced to the Hamidieh Barracks, which had been converted to a hospital. Nearly 12,000 Turkish soldiers thronged the barracks square and showed some fight. The 100-odd light-horsemen drew their swords and rode straight into the crowd. A few shots were fired, a few Turks were ridden down, and it was all over. With only one officer and three men wounded, Major Chanter had taken nearly 12,000 prisoners. Calm and confident, Chanter sent a galloper back to the regiment for help with the horde, then detached guards on the city's other hospitals and the Spanish consulate before the extra troops arrived.

Capture of the barracks solved a mystery. All along the line of the Turkish retreat, bodies had been scattered by the roadside. One trooper estimated that he had passed a body every 20 metres. The first men who entered the three-storey barracks building found that its hundreds of rooms were filled with beds, each one holding a dead Turkish soldier. They had died from pneumonic influenza. Now the highly infectious disease swept through the Desert Mounted Corps, so quickly that some units were unable continue the advance from Damascus. They did not have enough men to lead the horses of those sent to hospital. Dozens of men who had survived Gallipoli and the desert trails died in hospital beds on the eve of victory.

Even though German machine-gunners continued to offer pockets of resistance, the campaign was over to all intents and purposes. Fully half the remaining Turkish army had been lost at Damascus. Chauvel pushed the 5th Cavalry Division after the Turks but was forced to call a halt at Aleppo, his Indians and Yeomanry wasted by disease. He called up the weakened Australian Mounted Division, and they set out from Damascus on one last ride. They covered 156 kilometres in less than four days – 74 kilometres in the last 24 hours. Then, in an anticlimax, at Homs, north-east of Tripoli, they learnt that an armistice had been declared at noon on October 31 – a year to the day after the charge at Beersheba took place. The war in the east was over.

Trooper Fowler of the 12th Light Horse was one of the survivors. He said simply, "We were pleased to hear that the war had finished. As far as we were concerned it meant no more bullets or shells whistling around, and the finish of the long and weary rides. We were all too tired and weary to even talk much about the good news."

After a week of making do at Homs, the Australian Mounted Division rode to Tripoli, where they were welcomed by bagpipers and set up permanent camp on rolling hillsides overlooking the sea. Then on November 11 came the armistice with Germany and the end of the war. That night it rained and the signal flares that

LAWRENCE AND THE LIGHT HORSE

Colonel T.E. Lawrence stands with an escort of light-horsemen.

There was no love lost between the legendary Lawrence of Arabia and the Australian Light Horse. The Light Horse found Lawrence unreliable and his Arab force a band of plunderers. Lawrence in turn considered the Australians "thin-tempered, hollow, instinctive" and felt that the soldiers "had put off half civilization with their civil clothes."

Lawrence had first come to Palestine in 1910 as a scholar to study the castles of the Crusaders and subsequently returned to Syria on archeological and surveying work. He quickly mastered the Arabic language and dialects, and when Turkey entered World War I he was sent by British military intelligence to organise Arab resistance behind the Turkish lines.

Befriending Feisal, son of the Sherif of Mecca, Lawrence became were fired in celebration quickly spluttered to earth, leaving the light-horsemen with the darkness and their thoughts before they slept.

The months passed at Tripoli in training, which now seemed without purpose, and with sight-seeing tours to the Cedars of Lebanon, hearty sports meetings and time-killing lectures and classes. Captain Frank Hurley photographed each regiment, squadron by squadron. Some officers and men continued to die of disease. The 1914 "originals" were sent home, and the rest waited.

In November, the Light Horse and Mounted Rifles magazine *Kia Ora Coo-ee* confirmed a dismaying rumour that the horses were to stay behind. Gullett wrote: "We are told that to take them back would endanger the health of all Australian livestock, and further, that the cost of transport would be more than they are worth. More than they are worth! They are to be left behind and sold. Most of them are doubtless for the countries of the Mediterranean. The Mediterranean peoples have many attractive qualities, but I am sad to think they may get my old cuddy. Their way with horses is not ours."

Major Olden of the 10th Regiment was more direct: "Long experience of the native and his barbarous—at time hideously cruel—treatment of animals caused a universal shudder throughout Australian and New Zealand ranks at the mere thought of our gallant steeds in his possession."

As a massive wave of protest swept through the ranks, the idea of selling walers was dropped. Instead, in February 1919 the order was given that all horses would be classified A, B, C and D, according to age and condition. A and B class would go to Indian cavalry units; all C and D horses would be shot. They would have manes and tails shorn (for sale as horse hair) shoes removed (for recycling) and would be skinned. Army officialdom allowed three kilograms of salt for curing each hide.

A last race meeting was held, and then the horses were led away to olive groves outside Tripoli. There they were tethered in familiar picket lines, given a last nosebag, and shot by special squads of marksmen.

It was a dark hour for the light-horsemen. But within days they were shipped back to Egypt to begin preparations for their embarkation to

---

an active leader of the Arab Revolt against the Turks. In a brilliant operation, he captured Akaba in July 1917 and then began leading bands of Arab and Bedouin irregulars in raids on the Hejaz Railway. By now he had adopted Arab dress and was known to the Arabs as El Aurens.

Lawrence's Arab guerrillas were trained in the use of the Lewis gun by a light-horseman, Sergeant Charles Yells of the 3rd Machine-gun Squadron. Lawrence described Yells as "long, thin and sinuous, his supple body lounging in unmilitary curves. His hard face, arched eyebrows, and predatory nose set off the peculiarly Australian air of reckless willingness and capacity to do something very soon." He could not have given a better portrait of a Light Horse Billjim.

Less sympathetic was Lawrence's image of light-horsemen just before the fall of Damascus, when "the sporting Australians saw the campaign as a point-to-point, with Damascus as the post." Lawrence would be the loser in that race. After spending a night, anonymously dressed in Arab clothes, in a camp set up by Australians outside Damascus, he prepared to make his triumphal entrance next morning in his blue Rolls-Royce, sumptuous in gold and white robes. Some Indian lancers, under "an obtuse and bad-tempered" NCO, according to Lawrence, arrested him, and while Lawrence fumed, the Light Horse entered Damascus, accepted its surrender, and were first to receive the euphoric welcome of its people.

Lawrence's wartime activities were widely publicised after the war. Millions of people throughout the English-speaking world saw the lecture-and-slides show presented by the American journalist Lowell Thomas, which gave a colourful account of Lawrence's adventures. Lawrence himself wrote a flamboyant narrative of the events in *The Seven Pillars of Wisdom*.

At the height of his fame, however, Lawrence opted for obscurity and joined the RAF as a humble aircraftsman under an assumed name. Cynics said he "backed into the limelight." Allenby, his Commander-in-Chief in Palestine, is supposed to have told Lawrence: "In fifty years your name will be a household word; to find out about Allenby they will have to go to the War Museum." He was right. And he might well have added that people would think Lawrence beat the Light Horse into Damascus.

Australia. The 1st and 2nd Regiments set sail for home with bands playing, and the other regiments and brigades prepared to follow them. Then, in mid-March, the long-simmering rebellion erupted in Egypt. Fuelled by the end of the wartime boom and the forlorn hope of making Egyptian independence an issue at the Paris Peace Conference, the uprising merged with the death-throes of the jehad, the holy war against the infidel called by the Turkish Sultan in 1914.

By that time, almost all the British and Indian units of Allenby's army had been sent home. The British army in Egypt consisted of a small permanent garrison, the guards of prisoner-of-war camps and a few details. But the Light Horse were in their last month of sworn service to their Sovereign Lord the King. They were again mounted and equipped as cavalry and sent out to control the rebellion. Operating under the orders of British regional officers, they restored order and met violence with violence.

One rebel pamphlet urged the Egyptian people: "Prepare for them what you can, fight them with all that you can. Strike over the necks, split the heads, bury them in tombs alive, shower them with burned arrows whose flames they cannot extinguish. Give them to drink extremely hot water to cut their intestines and roast their livers." Inevitably, some light-horsemen were killed, and their mates retaliated. When a sentry was murdered, Ryrie ordered a village to surrender the man responsible. When there was no resonse, he burnt the village. A subaltern and 20 men were attacked by 1,000 rioters armed with sticks and stones. They opened fire. In a few minutes, 39 Egyptians were killed, 25 were wounded, and 40 drowned in trying to escape across a canal. Most of the casualties and much of the panic were probably caused when an aircraft fired two short bursts into the rioters. Rebels killed a number of British officers sightseeing on a train; some victims, alive or dead, were stuffed into the firebox of the locomotive. Shortly after this atrocity, several hundred Egyptians died in two pitched battles with light-horsemen.

Exuberant Egyptians celebrate in Cairo on April 7, 1919, after Allenby's announcement that deported leaders of the rebellion that broke out after the war were to be released. This decision saved Egypt for Britain for years to come.

THE HORSES STAY BEHIND

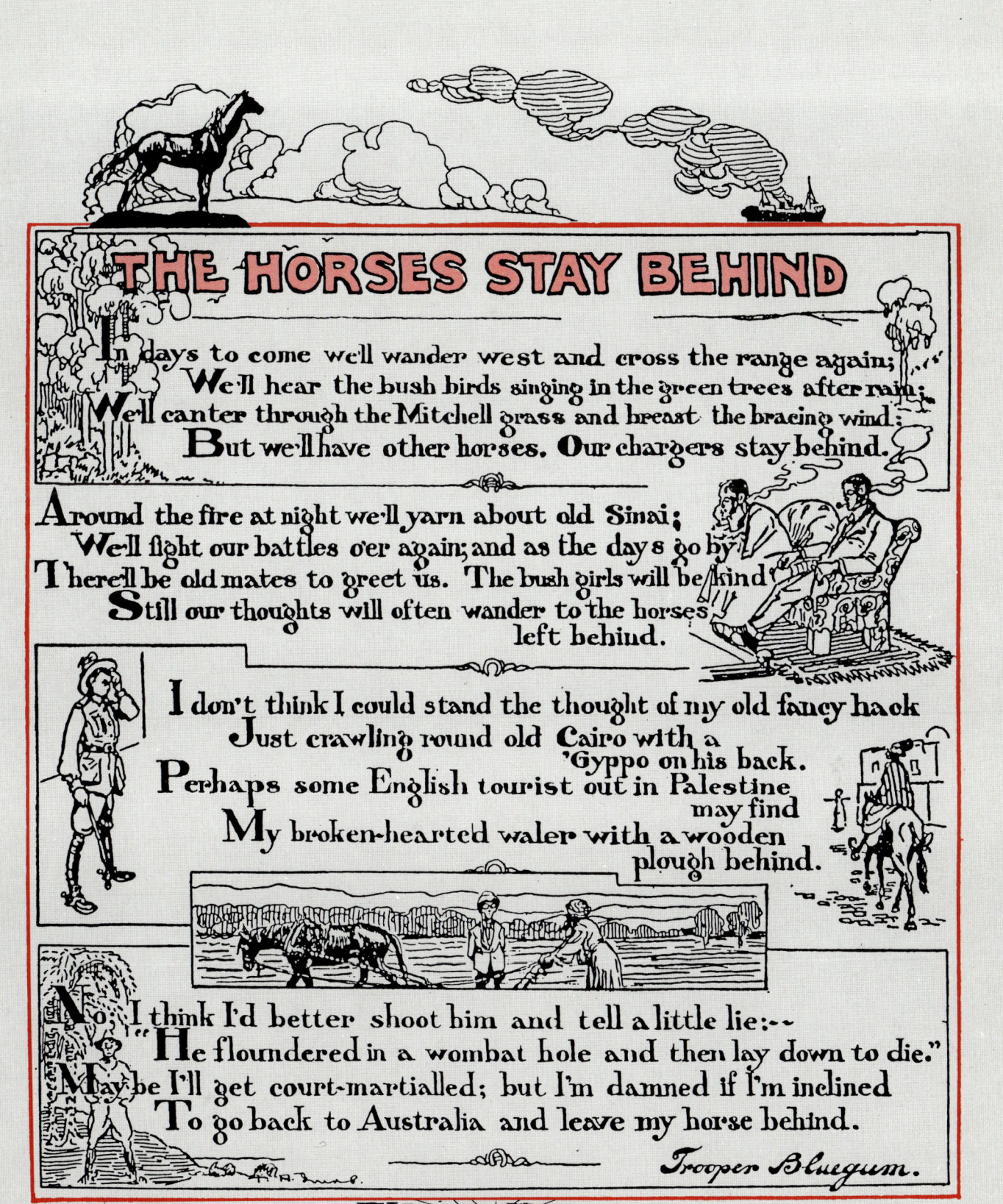

In days to come we'll wander west and cross the range again;
We'll hear the bush birds singing in the green trees after rain;
We'll canter through the Mitchell grass and breast the bracing wind;
But we'll have other horses. Our chargers stay behind.

Around the fire at night we'll yarn about old Sinai;
We'll fight our battles o'er again; and as the days go by
There'll be old mates to greet us. The bush girls will be kind
Still our thoughts will often wander to the horses left behind.

I don't think I could stand the thought of my old fancy hack
Just crawling round old Cairo with a 'Gyppo on his back.
Perhaps some English tourist out in Palestine may find
My broken-hearted waler with a wooden plough behind.

No, I think I'd better shoot him and tell a little lie:—
"He floundered in a wombat hole and then lay down to die."
Maybe I'll get court-martialled; but I'm damned if I'm inclined
To go back to Australia and leave my horse behind.

Trooper Bluegum.

In a little more than a month, the rebellion was over and Allenby ruled Egypt. Three months before, he had sharply criticised Australians and New Zealanders for a bloody reprisal against the Arabs of Surafend in Palestine after the murder of a New Zealander. Now, he bade farewell to the Light Horse with a remarkable tribute: "The Australian lighthorseman combines with a splendid physique a restless activity of mind. This mental quality renders him somewhat impatient of rigid and formal discipline, but it confers upon him the gift of adaptability, and this is the secret of much of his success mounted or on foot. In this dual role ... the Australian light-horseman has proved himself equal to the best. He has earned the gratitude of the Empire and the admiration of the world."

The Light Horse buried the last of their dead, surrendered their new horses, handed in their gear and, at last, embarked for Australia in a succession of transports over the next couple of months. After a four-week voyage, they approached the coast of Western Australia. Some had been away for four years. "We looked and strained our eyes for some time," said a trooper, "and some men climbed up into the rigging of the ship to get a better view, and then we could see the faint outline of those desolate hills, and some war-hardened men turned away to hide the tears that came into their eyes."

The regiments broke up, the men scattered throughout the states of the Commonwealth. No homecoming was typical. Harry Bostock's was just one among the 5,000-odd that took place in that second half of 1919. His parents, brother, two aunts and a cousin met him at the Fremantle wharf. "I made a bee-line for my dear mother for a long hug, with tears of emotion in our eyes." Then came the trip home to Staunton Springs near Pingelly, Western Australia. "At the house gate was a 'Welcome Home' banner with my faithful old Border Collie dog Toby beneath it. . . . It only took about ten minutes or less and then he became very excited, running around me and then took a flying leap to my chest, as he had done in the past. After that, he never left me. What a wonderful memory a dog has, and why should he have howled all night the time I was wounded. . . .

"For a little time after my return I didn't do very much, except visit the relatives of those killed in action. . . . After that I made a final trip to Perth for my discharge from the A.I.F. and then I was glad to settle down to the old routine of farm life. I loved it, driving and caring for a team of horses once more."

The Light Horse of the 1st AIF existed for only five years; the AIF as a whole was officially disbanded on April 1, 1921. Citizen Military Forces Light Horse units thrived in the 1920s and declined in the Depression years of the 1930s when horses became an expensive luxury. Some CMF Light Horse regiments were motorised before the outbreak of World War II in 1939. The last were dismounted in the second year of the war. The Light Horse had vanished as everything but a proud title carried by Australian armoured units through World War II, Korea and Vietnam.

Historian Bill Gammage read scores of lighthorsemen's diaries and letters before reaching his conclusion: "The fierce individuality with which he fought Turks, Arabs, and English staff officers lay close to the heart of the Australian light horseman. He lived under few restraints and was equally careless of man, God and nature. Yet he stood by his own standards firmly, remaining brave in battle, loyal to his mates, generous to the Turks, and pledged to his King and country. His speech betrayed few of his enthusiasms, and he accepted success and failure equally without demonstration, but the confident dash of the horseman combined with the practical resource and equanimity of the bushman in him, and moved him alike over the wilderness of Sinai and the hills of the Holy Land. Probably his kind will not be seen again, for the conditions of war and peace and romance that produced him have almost entirely disappeared."

Sitting proudly astride his waler, this trooper in full array exemplifies the Light Horse of the first AIF, which existed for only five years but created an undying legend.

BIBLIOGRAPHY

Adam Smith, Patsy. *The Anzacs.* Melbourne: Nelson, 1978.
Bean, C.E.W. *Anzac to Amiens.* Canberra: Australian War Memorial, 1946.
Bean, C.E.W., ed. *Official History of Australia in the War of 1914-1918.* Sydney: Angus & Robertson, 1921-43.
  Vols 1 and 2, *The Story of Anzac,* by C.E.W. Bean, 1921, 1924.
  Vol. 7, *The Australian Imperial Force in Sinai and Palestine,* by H.S. Gullett, 1923.
  Vol. 12, *Photographic Record of the War,* annotated by C.E.W. Bean and H.S. Gullett, 1923.
Bolton, Sloan. *A Dream of the Past.* Privately printed, n.d.
Bostock, Henry P. *The Great Ride.* Perth: Artlook, 1982.
Brugger, Suzanne. *Australians in Egypt, 1914-1919.* Carlton, Vic.: Melbourne University Press, 1980.
Butler, A.G., ed. *Official History of the Australian Army Medical Services in the War of 1914-1918.* Vol. 1. Melbourne: Australian War Memorial, 1930.
Changing of the Guard, The. Canberra: Australian War Memorial, 1944.
Devitt, Napier. *Galloping Jack.* London: Witherby, 1937.
Elliott, E.G. "The 4th L.H. Brigade Cavalry Charge at Beersheba." Typescript. Melbourne, 1967.
Ellis, John. *Cavalry.* New York: Putnam, 1978.
Falls, Cyril. *Military Operations, Egypt and Palestine.* London, 1930.
Firkins, Peter. *The Australians in Nine Wars.* Adelaide: Rigby, 1971.
Fowler, J.E. *Looking Backward.* Aranda, ACT: Roebuck Society, 1979.
Gammage, Bill. *The Broken Years.* Canberra: Australian National University Press, 1974.
Gardner, Brian. *Allenby.* London: Cassell, 1965.
Gullett, H.S., Charles Barrett, and David Barker, eds. *Australia in Palestine.* Sydney: Angus & Robertson, 1919.
Hall, Rex. *The Desert Hath Pearls.* Melbourne: Hawthorn Press, 1975.
Hall, R.J. *The Australian Light Horse.* Blackburn, Vic.: W.D. Joynt, 1968.
Hamerton, J.A. *A Popular History of the Great War.* London, n.d.
Hamilton, Patrick. "Riders of Destiny." Microfiche. Melbourne, 1985.
Harding, Bruce. *Windows of Fame.* Melbourne: Lansdowne, 1963.
Hill, A.J. *Chauvel of the Light Horse.* Carlton, Vic.: Melbourne University Press, 1978.
History of the First World War, vol. 2, no. 10, "Forcing the Narrows." London: BPC Publishing, 1970.
Hogue, Oliver. *Trooper Bluegum at the Dardanelles.* London: Melrose, 1916.
——. *The Cameliers.* London: Melrose, 1919.
Hussein Husni Amir Bey. "Yilderim." Translated by C.O. de R. Channer. Typescript, n.d.
Idriess, Ion L. *The Desert Column.* Sydney: Angus & Robertson, 1933.
Kempe, Humphrey, *Participation.* Melbourne: Hawthorn Press, 1973.
Keogh, E.G. *Suez to Alleppo.* Melbourne: Military Board, 1955.
Laffin, John. *Anzacs at War.* London: Abelard-Schuman, 1965.
Lawrence, T.E. *The Seven Pillars of Wisdom.* London: Jonathan Cape, 1926.
——. *Revolt in the Desert.* London: Jonathan Cape, 1927.
Lloyd George, David. *War Memoirs.* London: Nicholson & Watson, 1933-36.
Massey, W.T. *The Desert Campaigns.* London: Constable, 1918.
——. *How Jerusalem Was Won.* London: Constable, 1919.
——. *Allenby's Final Triumph.* London: Constable, 1920.
Meinertzhagen, Richard. *Middle East Diary, 1917-1956.* London: Cresset Press, 1959.
Mitchell, Elyne. *Light Horse.* Melbourne: Macmillan, 1978.
Mitchell, Gregory. *The Bush Horseman.* Sydney: Reed, 1981.
Morris, James. *Farewell the Trumpets.* Harmondsworth, Middx.: Penguin, 1981.
Nogales, Rafael de. *Four Years beneath the Crescent.* London: Scribner's, 1926.
Olden, A.C.N. *Westralian Cavalry in the War.* Melbourne: McCubbin, 1921.
Paterson, A.B. ("Banjo"). *Happy Dispatches.* Sydney: Angus & Robertson, 1934.
Pirie-Gordon, H. *A Brief Record of the Advance of the Egyptian Expeditionary Force.* Cairo: Palestine News, 1919.
Preston, R.M.P. *The Desert Mounted Corps.* London: Constable, 1921.
Sanders, Liman von. *Five Years in Turkey.* London: Bailliere, Tindal and Cox, 1928.
Smith, Cyril. "Beersheba." Privately printed, n.d.
Stanley, Peter, and Michael McKernan. *Australians at War, 1885-1972.* Sydney: Collins, 1984.
Sutherland, L.W. *Mementoes of the 1st Squadron, Australian Flying Corps, 1914-1918.* Royal Australian Air Force Association, Sydney.
Tuohy, Ferdinand. *The Secret Corps.* London: Murray, 1920.
United States Cavalry School. *History of the Palestine Campaign.* Kansas, 1923.
Vernon, P. V., ed. *The Royal New South Wales Lancers, 1885-1985.* Parramatta, NSW: Royal New South Wales Lancers Centenary Committee, 1986.
Wavell, A.P. *The Palestine Campaigns.* London: Constable, 1928.
Wilson, L.C. "The Third L.H. Brigade A.I.F. in the Egyptian Rebellion, 1919." Typescript. Brisbane, 1934.

ACKNOWLEDGMENTS

For their help in the preparation of this book, the author and publishers wish to thank the staff of the Australian War Memorial, Canberra, especially Dr Michael McKernan, Peter Burness, Bill Fogarty, Geoff McKeown, Peter Aitken, Bryan Butler, George Imashev, Ian Affleck, Steve Corvini, Andrew Jack, Peter West, Beryl Strusz, Anne Gray, Stewart James and Eva Johns; also Colonel P.V. Vernon of the Royal New South Wales Lancers Memorial Museum, Parramatta. The author's special thanks go to Colonel E.G. Keogh, for his shrewd tactical assessments of the Light Horse campaigns; Alec Hill, for generous advice and for his invaluable biography of Chauvel; and the many light-horsemen who shared their memories with him, in particular Clive Newman of the 9th Light Horse Regiment, who visited the Nek with him, and Ted Eardley of the 11th Regiment, who was with him at Shell Green and Beersheba, and the many friends of the 4th Regiment, including Heyden Ewart, Lindsay Taylor, Vic Smith, Jack Taggart, Bill Scott, Fenton Denny and Dave Chambers.

PICTURE CREDITS

Credits from left to right are separated by semicolons, from top to bottom by oblique strokes. AWM = Australian War Memorial.

COVER and page 1: AWM B1492

THE LEGEND BEGINS. 6-7: AWM A4955. 8: AWM A4953 / A4947. 9: AWM A5081 / A5238. 10-11: AWM A4337; A5234 / A5305; A4881. 12: AWM 129022 / A4293. 13: AWM 129017. 14: AWM A4942. 15: AWM A5315.

RAW BRIGADES. 16: AWM 2758. 19: AWM B10. 21: AWM J450. 22: Courtesy Bob Leonard, Westpac, Sydney. 27: Courtesy RAAF Association, Sydney / map by Wendy Gorton. 29: AWM 430. 31: AWM 7965.

SADDLING UP FOR WAR. 32-33: AWM J328. 34: AWM H11585. 35: AWM J320 / A142. 36: AWM J95 / J339. 37: AWM J343. 38, 39: AWM A1288 / C3524 / A1283; J333. 40: AWM A178 / A176. 41: AWM A180. 42, 43: AWM A3893; C2482 / A1237.

THE DESERT COLUMN. 44: AWM, loose sheet 351. 46-47: AWM PS 913. 47: AWM G1478; B2908 / C497; C3460. 48: map by Wendy Gorton. 50: AWM A2910. 53: AWM 9556. 55: Courtesy RAAF Association, Sydney / State Library of NSW. 56-57: AWM B1627. 59: AWM A225 / Courtesy RAAF Association, Sydney. 61: AWM J6559. 63: AWM J2473. 64: AWM B2001.

SURVIVING IN THE DESERT. 66-67: AWM B2970. 68-69: AWM A2994 / B2976. 70: AWM A627 / A2405. 71: AWM B1610. 72-73: AWM B26. 74: AWM A1631 / A5015. 75: AWM J5984 / Courtesy RAAF Association, Sydney. 76. 77: AWM B142; Courtesy Lt-Col. P. V. Vernon, Sydney. 78: Courtesy Mr and Mrs Steel, Auckland / AWM J5259. 79: Courtesy Mr and Mrs Steel, Auckland. 80-81: AWM J1122, 82: AWM A221. 83: Reproduced from *The Changing of the Guard* / AWM B2714. 84-85: AWM C2924; J3178 / C2921; B1770.

THE CHARGE AT BEERSHEBA. 86: AWM, loose sheet 300. 88, 89: Map by Wendy Gorton; AWM B1623. 91: AWM H10707 / Courtesy RAAF Association, Sydney. 93: Courtesy estate of Malcolm Morrow, Sydney. 94-95: Drawings by Charles Goodwin, 97: AWM J6568. 99: Map by Wendy Gorton. 100-101: AWM A2684. 103: AWM 2811.

SHOT IN COLOUR. 105: AWM B1650. 106: AWM B1697. 107: AWM B1689. 108-109: AWM B1624. 110: AWM B1662 / B1700. 111: AWM B1727. 112: AWM B1664 113: AWM B1686.

DEADLOCK IN THE EAST. 114: AWM, loose sheet 292. 116: Map by Wendy Gorton. 117: AWM B1456. 119: AWM A2053 / B2971. 120-121: Reproduced from *The Changing of the Guard*. 122-123: AWM B1450. 124: AWM A2510. 125: Courtesy estate of Malcolm Morrow, Sydney. 127: AWM B10. 128-129: AWM B1619. 131: Map by Wendy Gorton. 132: AWM B67. 133: Courtesy estate of Malcolm Morrow, Sydney. 134: AWM B36 / Courtesy estate of Malcolm Morrow, Sydney.

THE NEW MACHINES OF WAR. 136-137: AWM B54. 138: AWM A315. 139: AWM B707 / C2602. 140-141: AWM B1575 / B2864; A226. 142: AWM B1959 / A628. 143: Reproduced from *The Changing of the Guard* / AWM 1363. 144-145: B2475 / B418.

THE GREAT RIDE. 146: AWM, loose sheet 310. 149: Map by Wendy Gorton. 150: Courtesy RAAF Association, Sydney. 151: AWM B259. 153: AWM B277. 156: AWM 9755. 158: AWM J6569. 160: Courtesy estate of Malcolm Morrow, Sydney. 161: Reproduced from *Australia in Palestine*. 163: Courtesy Lt-Col. P. V. Vernon, Sydney.

INDEX

Numerals in italics indicate an illustration of the subject mentioned.

A
Abd, Bir el, 53, 54
Abu Tellul, *map* 131, 133, 135
Aleppo, *map* 48, 158
Ali Muntar, 60, 61, 62, 63, 64
Allenby, General Sir Edmund, 18, 19, *91*, 93, 124; and capture of Jerusalem, 118, *120*, 122; rebuilds army and plans Palestine strategy, 127, 146-148, 154; his tribute to Light Horse, 162
Amman, *map* 48, 124, 126, *map* 149, 152
Antill, Brigadier-General J.M., 24, 30, 52-53
Anzac Cove, 26, *map* 27. *See also* Gallipoli
Anzac Mounted Division, organisation of, 24, 49, 60, 90. *See also* Australian Light Horse; New Zealand Mounted Rifles Brigade
Arab Revolt, 124, 159
Arabs, 87, 89, *119*, 126, 152-153, 159; Senussi, 56
Arish, El, 45, *map* 48, 54
Armoured cars, *136-137*, 138, *139*, *140-141*
Ashdod, *107*
Asluj, *map* 48, *map* 88, 89, 90, 93
Australian army, formation of, 18. *See also* Australian Imperial Force
Australian Camel Corps, 56. *See also* Imperial Camel Corps Brigade
Australian Flying Corps, *105*, 138, *142*, *143*, *150*, 152
Australian Imperial Force, 17, 20, 25. *See also* Australian Light Horse
Australian Light Horse: formation, command and composition of, 17, 18-19, 20, 22, 24, 147; equipment and uniform, 19, 22, 23, *94-95*, 147; recruitment and training, 19-20, *33-41*; departure and voyage to Egypt, 22-23, *42-43*; training and activities in Egypt, 23-25, *46-47*; at Gallipoli, 26-31; regroup in Egypt, 45; at Romani-Katia, 45, 50-53, *74*, *84*; at Magdhaba, 54-58, 59; at Gaza, 61-62, 64, 65; and Beersheba, 93, 96, 97, 98-104; at Sheria, 115-117; in Judaean Hills, 118-119; and capture of Jerusalem, 119-120; and capture of Jericho, *122-123*, 124; and attack on Amman, 126; and attack on Es Salt, 127, *128-129*, 130-133; in Jordan Valley, 133-135; begin the Great Ride, 148; at Jenin and Nablus, 150, *151*; capture Amman and Es Salt, 152; and Ziza incident, 152-153; at Semakh, 154; and drive to Damascus, 155-157; pursue Turks to Homs, 158; and Egyptian rebellion, 160-162; return to Australia, 162. *See also* Light-horsemen; Horses
Australian Mounted Division: formation of, 24, 90; issued with swords, 147. *See also* Australian Light Horse; Imperial Mounted Division
Australian War Memorial, 106

B
Baghdad, 87
Barada Gorge, *156*, 157
Bean, C.E.W., 30
Bedouin. *See* Arabs
Beersheba, *map* 48, 60, *map* 88, 88-89, 92, 93-104, *map* 99, 114; charge at, *16-17*, 19, 98-104, *map* 99, *100-101*, *103*
Belah, *71*, 122
Bethlehem, *map* 116, 123
Black Hill, 131, *map* 131, 132
Bluff, the, *map* 131, 135
Boer War, *6-15*, 17-18, 50, 55
Bostock, Trooper Henry, 59, 87, 121, 129, 162
Bourchier, Lieutenant-Colonel M.W., 90, 98, 99, 103, 121, 123; strike force of, 155-156; at Damascus, 157
Bridges, Major-General Sir William Throsby, 20, 21
Brierty, Lieutenant A.R., 117
British army: in Cairo, 25; at Gaza, 62, 65; Indian troops, 120, 127, 147; at Jerusalem, 120; at Rafa, 58; reorganised, 127; at Romani-Katia area, 45-49, 51, 52; Scottish infantry, 45, 49, *119*, 121; at Sheria, 115-117; 60th Division (Londoners), 115, 117, 119, 120, 123, 124, 126; Yeomanry Mounted Division, 24, 90
Broadmeadows camp, *32-33*, 34, *37*, *39*
Burj, El, 119
Bushmen (at Boer War), *6-7*, *8*, *10*, *12*, 17-18

C
Cairo, 23, 25, *160*
Camel Corps, *See* Imperial Camel Corps Brigade
Camels, *56-57*, *84*, 120, 124-125; ambulance, *108-109*
Camel's Hump, the, 57
Cameron, Lieutenant-Colonel Donald, 98, 99, 115, 152
Casualties: at Amman and Es Salt, 126, 133; at Beersheba, 104; in Boer War, 15; enemy, 47, 54, 59, 60, 63, 154; first Australian, in Sinai, 45; on Gallipoli, 30, 31; at Gaza, 63, 65; at Jericho, 124; at Rafa, 60; at Semakh, 154; of Yeomanry, near Huj, 118
Chanter, Major J.C., 157
Chauvel, Lieutenant-General Sir Harry (Henry George), 23, 45, *55*; at Boer War, 9, 18; at Gallipoli, 31; and Romani-Katia action, 49-54; and attacks on Magdhaba and Rafa, 54-58; knighted, 60; and first Gaza, 61, 62; given command of Desert Column, 86; leads Desert Mounted Corps, 90; and battle of Beersheba, 97, 98; and third Gaza, 115; at Sheria, 115, 117; and attack on Shunet Nimrin and Es Salt, 127; and Great Drive, 148, 150, 154, 155
Chaytor, Major-General E.J., 51, 52, 62, 153
Cheape, Lieutenant-Colonel, H.A., 117
Chetwode, Lieutenant-General Sir Phillip, 54, 86; and Beersheba, 96, 97; and first Gaza, 60, 61, 62; and plan for capture of Gaza, 89; and Rafa action, 58-60
Chunuk Bair, *map* 27, 28, 31
Cook, Joseph, 19
Cox, Brigadier-General C.F., 54, 58, *123*, 135
Cyclist Battalion, 45, *139*

D
Dallas, Major-General G.A., 60, 61, 62, 63
Damascus, *map* 48, 55, *map* 149, 154-155, 157-158, 159
Damieh Bridge, 129, 130, *map* 131
Dead Sea, 123, *map* 131
Deraa, *map* 48, *map* 149, 152, 154-155
Desert, survival in, *66-85*
Desert Column: Chauvel given command of, 86; composition and formation of, 24, 54
Desert Mounted Corps, composition and formation of, 24, 90
Djemal Pasha, 47
Dobell, Lieutenant-General Sir Charles, 54, 60, 61, 62, 63, 86
Doig, Lieutenant P.W., 150
Donkeys, 120
Dueidar, 45, 49
Dunbar, Chaplain W.J. 117
Duntroon, 36

E

Eastern Force, 54, 63. *See also* British army
Edib Bey, Lieutenant-Colonel, 62
Egypt: British protectorate established, 25; rebellion in, 25, 160-162
Egyptians, Light Horse opinions of, 25, 119
Egyptian Transport Corps and Labour Corps, 119, 120
Elands River post, 8
Emu plumes, 19
Esani, *map* 88, 93
Esdraelon Plain, 148, *map* 149, 150

F

Falkenhayn, General Erich von, 86-87, 131
Fevsi Pasha, 115
Fitzgerald, Brigadier-General P.D., 98
Forsyth, Lieutenant-General J.K., 20-22, 23, 24-25, 26, 45
Foulkes-Taylor, Lieutenant Charles, 130
Fowler, Trooper J.E., 65, 102, 119, 132, 154, 155-156
French Troops, 24, 147, 152, 156

G

Galilee, Sea of, 153, 154
Gallipoli, 25-31, 45
Gas shells, 63, 64
Gaza, *map* 48, *map* 88, *map* 116, *117*; first battle, 60-63; second battle, 63, 64; third battle, 92, 115
Ghoraniye, 124, 125, *map* 131, bridgehead, *127*
Girheir, El, *map* 88, 92
Grant, Brigadier-General William, 98, 129, 130-133, 154
Granville, Lieutenant-Colonel C.H., 135

H

Halja, 125
Hall, Captain Rex, 126, 151-152, 156
Hamidieh Barracks, 157, 158
Hamilton, General Sir Ian, 26
Hamisah, Bir el, 52
Hareira, 115, *map* 116
Hejaz Railway, *map* 48, 124, *map* 131, 159
Heliopolis, 23
Hindhaugh, Major Jack, 23, 45
Hodgson, Major-General H.W., 60, 97, 98, 148, 151
Hods, 68, *70, 71*

Hogue, Major Oliver, 28, 31, 152, 156; verse by, 57, *161*
Homs, *map* 48, 158
Horses: care of, 23, 68; equipment of, 20, *94-95*; left behind, 159, *161*; qualities of, 21, 82, 83; ration for, 76; training of, 24, *38*
Horses, dummy, *134*, 135, 147
Hotchkiss gun, *63*-64
Hughes, Colonel G.F., 23, 50
Huj, 115, *map* 116
Hurley, Captain J.F., 106, *113*, 122, 159; photographs by, *105-113*
Hutton, Major-General Sir Edward, 18

I

Idriess, Trooper Ion L., 53, 61-62, 65
Imperial Camel Corps Brigade, 24, 54, *56-57*, 90; at Magdhaba, 58; at Rafa, 59, 60; at Gaza, 65; and Moab plateau, 124, 126; disbanded, 147
Imperial Mounted Division, 24, 60, 61, 64, 89-90. *See also* Australian Light Horse; Australian Mounted Division
Ismet Bey, Lieutenant-Colonel, 89, 92, 96-97, 98, 102

J

Jaffa, *map* 48, 147, 148, *map* 149
Jemel Pasha, 130
Jemmameh, Wadi, *map* 116, 118
Jenin, *map* 149, 150, *151*
Jericho, 123-124, *map* 131
Jerusalem, *map* 48, *111*, *map* 116, 119-120
Jifjafa, 45, *map* 48, 82
Jordan River, pontoon bridges across, 124, *125*
Jordan Valley, 68, *75*, 123, 133, *map* 149
Judaean Hills, 56, 118-119, 121, *map* 149
Junction Station, *map* 116, 118, *map* 149

K

Kantara, 45, *map* 48, 51
Karm, 114, 115, *map* 116
Katia, 45, *map* 48, 50, 52, 53, 54
Kaukab Ridge, *map* 149, 155, 156,
Kempe, Trooper Humphrey, 26-28, 50, 53-54, 115
Khalasa, *map* 88, 90, 93
Khuweilfeh, 115, *map* 116
Kia Ora Coo-ee, 119, 159
Kressenstein, Major-General Kress von, 49-50, 54, 131; and Beersheba attack, 92, 96; at Gaza, 60, 62, 63, 115
Kuneitra, *map* 48, *map* 149, 155

L

Labyrinth, the, 61, 64
Lambert, George, W., 21; paintings by, *31, 53, 156*; sketches by, *16, 44, 86, 114, 146*
Lawrence, Major-General H.A., 49, 50, 51, 52, 54
Lawrence, Colonel T.E., 90, 124, 126, 152, 157, *158-159*
Lawson, Major James, 102, 103
Light Car Patrol. *See* Armoured cars
Light-horsemen: background of, 19; descriptions of, 119, 158, 159, 162; join other branches of service, 45, 138, 139; qualities and requirements of, 17-18; relations with British troops, 49, 119, 126; relations with Egyptians and Arabs, 25, 119, 126. *See also* Australian Light Horse
Lloyd George, David, 63
Lone Pine, *map* 27, 28, 30

M

Maadi, 23
Ma'an, *map* 48, 152
Magdhaba, *map* 48, 54-58, *59*
Maghara, *map* 48, 54
Magruntein, El, 59, 60
Massey, W.T., 25, 157
Maxwell, General Sir John, 25, 26, 44
Mazar, 54
Mecca, Sherif of, 124, 158
Megiddo, 148, *map* 149, 150
Meinertzhagen, Major Richard, 90, 92
Mena Camp, 23, 25
Meredith, Colonel J.B., 50
Meridith, Mount, 51, *66-67*
Moab plateau, 124, 126, 127, 129, *map* 131
Monaghan, Corporal S.F., 45
Monash Valley, 26, *map* 27, 28
Munro-Ferguson, Sir Ronald, *22*
Murray, General Sir Archibald, 44, 45, 49, 54, 60; and Gaza, 60, 63, 86; replaced, 90
Musmus Pass *map* 149, 150
Mussalabeh, 57, *map* 131, 133, *134*

N

Nablus, 129, *map* 149, 151
Nazareth, 148, *map* 149, 153
Nek, the, 26, *map* 27, 28-31

167

New South Wales Citizen Bushmen, 8, 9
New South Wales Lancers, 11, 18
New South Wales Mounted Rifles, *10-11*
New Zealand Mounted Rifles Brigade, 24, 45, 49; at Beersheba, 96, 97; and capture of Jericho, 123; at Gaza, 62, 65; in Jordan Valley, 124; at Romani-Katia, 51, 52, 53, 54. *See also* Australian Light Horse
Nimrin, Wadi, *83*

O
Oghratina, 45, *map* 48
Olden, Lieutenant-Colonel A.G., 118, 120, 150, 157
Omrah (transport), *43*
Onslow, Brigadier-General George Macarthur, 96, 156

P
Palestine: conditions in, 68; Light Horse enter, 60; as Turkish possession, 25
Paterson, Major A.B. ("Banjo"), 78, 90, 97
Patterson, Lieutenant R.R.W., 151
Philistine plain, *88*
Pope's Hill, 31
Prisoners, German, 135
Prisoners, Turkish: at Damascus, 157; at Es Salt, 132; during Great Ride, 152, 153, 154; at Jenin, 150, 151; at Jifjafa, 45; at Magdhaba, 58, *59*; at Nablus, 152; at Romani-Katia, 52 54; after Suez raid, 44, *47*

Q
Queensland Mounted Infantry, 8, 9, 18, 19, 20
Quinn's Post, 26, *map* 27, 31

R
Rae, Major Norman, 155
Rafa, *map* 48, 57, 58-60, 108
Railway, British military, 45, 60, 63, 92
Red Crescent, 25, *84*
Remounts. *See* Horses
Rickaby, Lieutenant T.N., 87, 120
Roberts, Lord, 8, 18
Robertson, Major Horace, 58
Romani, 45, *map* 48, 49, *68-69, 74*; battle of 50-52, 53, *66-67, 84*
Royston, Brigadier-General J.R., 49, *50*, 87, 93; at Gaza, 62, 65, at Magdhaba, 58; at Rafa, 59; at Romani-Katia, 51-54
Royston, Mount, 51, 52
Russell's Top, *map* 27, 30
Ryrie, Colonel Granville, 24, 28, 31, 93, 124; and Beersheba, 96; and Egyptian rebellion, 160; and first Gaza, 62; at Romani-Katia, 45, 49; at Ziza, 153

S
Saba, Tel el, *map* 88, 96, 97
Saba, Wadi, 88, 102
Sakati, Tel el, *map* 88, 96
Salt, Es, *map* 48, 124, 126, 127, 129-133, *map* 131, 152
Sanders, General Liman von, 131, 147, 153
Sasa, *map* 149, 155
Schiller, Captain, 92
Scott, Major W.H., 45
Semakh, *map* 149, 154
Senussi Arabs, 56
Shanahan, Major M., 50-51
Shell Green, 26, *map* 27, 28
Sheria, *map* 88, 92, 115-117, *map* 116
Shrapnel Gully, 26, *27*
Shunet Nimrim, 127, 130, *map* 131
Sinai, campaign in, 44-60; conditions in, 49, 68; crossed by Turks, 44, 47

Sing, Trooper W.E., 28
Smith, Brigadier-General C.L., 62
Smith, Captain Ross, 106, *143*
Snipers, 28, *29, 110*
South Australian Imperial Bushmen, *6-7, 8, 14*
Steele's Post, 26, *map* 27
Stopford, General Sir Frederick, 28
Suez Canal, Turkish attack on, 44, *46-47*
Suvla Bay, *map* 27, 28, 31

T
Table Top, 131, *map* 131
Tala Bey, 63
Tanks, 63, 64, 65, 138, *141*
Temptation, Mount of, *133*
Throssell, Lieutenant Hugo, 65
Tiberias, *map* 149, 153
Turkey: calls for holy war, 25; war declared on, 23

W
Wahaby, Bey, 152, 153
Walers. *See* Horses
War, declaration of, 18-19, 22-23
Water pipeline, 45, 60, 92, *map* 116
Water supply: in Palestine, 87-88, 90, 93, 114, 118; in Sinai, 49, 68
Wellington Ridge, 51, 52
Wilson, Brigadier-General Lachlan, 93, 129, 130
Wiltshire (transport), 23
Wozza, Battle of the, 25

Y
Yeomanry. *See* British army
Yilderim, 89, 103, 130

Z
Ziza, *map* 149, 152-153